What is Britannica Smart

Encyclopædia Britannica® has worked with educational experts to develop an online adaptive practice product that will encourage and challenge your child to become better in math. *Britannica SmartMath®* has an extensive math curriculum and the program will automatically create individualized learning paths for your child. The program will track your child's strengths and weaknesses in different topics from Grades 1 through 6 and will choose appropriate materials for your child's practice sessions.

The *Britannica SmartMath®* workbook series has been integrated with the online learning program. When a workbook section is completed, your child can earn points that can be applied to the online learning system—allowing the online program to carry your child's math learning to the next level!

35,000 Math Problems
91 Math Topics
Grade 1-6
5 Dimensions in Math

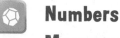 **Numbers**
Measures
Shapes and Space
Data Handling
Algebra

1 Quality Math Content

SmartMath content is aligned with the National Council of Teachers of Mathematics standards. All activities are aimed to help your child build solid foundations in five math areas: Numbers, Measures, Shapes and Space, Data Handling, and Algebra.

2 Online Exercises that Adapt to Your Child

Learning math is more personalized than ever because the *SmartMath®* program tracks your child's strengths and weaknesses in different topics and intuitively adapts the presented material accordingly.

3 Motivated Self-Learning

Britannica SmartMath® wants to make math practice an enjoyable experience. In addition to the special characters and user-friendly interface, children are naturally motivated with special reward badges, progress certificates, and a web leader board.

Program Features

Introducing Britannica SmartMath: the world's most advanced math practice system!

DESIGNED FOR THE INDIVIDUAL CHILD!

A little practice every day goes a long way in mathematics. SmartMath makes it easy, interactive, and enjoyable for your child.

▶ **SmartMath Core**
Browse the extensive library of quality math practice questions

▶ **Explore It!**
Explore math concepts with our interactive manipulatives

▶ **My Badges**
Track achievements by topic and print certificates

▶ **My Points & Leader Board**
Earn points on the monthly leader board to encourage self-learning

SMARTMATH IS PARENT-FRIENDLY!

Stay informed about your child's math progress at the convenience of a click. The more you know, the more you can help your child succeed and move to the next level!

▶ **Calendar View**
Monitor your child's login information & practice time

▶ **Report Card**
View your child's progress within each math topic

▶ **Curriculum View**
Track your child's progress according to our curriculum

▶ **Worldwide Comparison!**
Compare your child's progress to other users

▶ **Send Messages**
Personalize words of encouragement and feedback for your child

Practice for Exams!

Varied questions help improve your child's skills in multiple areas: number sense, understanding word problems, logical reasoning, and concept application.

Practice Anytime!

Choose relevant topics and allow your child to practice new math skills while reinforcing critical skills learned at school – just 15 to 30 minutes each day will go a long way!

Practice Wisely!

The SmartMath system tracks your child's success within each math topic. Practice is designed to capitalize on learning strengths and build confidence in weaker areas.

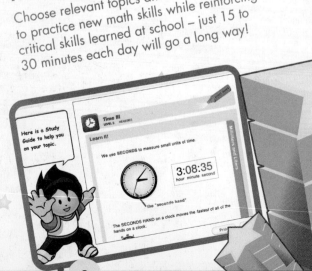

SMARTMATH Curriculum Levels, Dimensions, and Math Topics

Level 1

NUMBERS
- **10** Numbers to 10
- **20** Numbers to 20
- **+/−** Basic Addition & Subtraction
- **100** Numbers to 100
- **+/− 12** Addition & Subtraction I

MEASURES
- **$** Money I
- **🕐** Time I
- **📏** Length & Distance I
- **📏 cm** Length & Distance II

SHAPES AND SPACE
- Straight Lines & Curved Lines
- 2-D Shapes
- 3-D Shapes

Level 2

NUMBERS
- **999** 3-Digit Numbers
- **+/− 123** Addition & Subtraction II
- **+/− 456** Addition & Subtraction III
- **99999** 4-Digit Numbers
- **×** Basic Multiplication
- **÷** Basic Division

MEASURES
- **⊙** Money II
- **🕐** Time II
- **📏 m** Length & Distance III
- **📐** Weight

SHAPES AND SPACE
- Quadrilaterals I
- Angles I
- 3-D Shapes II
- The Four Compass Points

DATA HANDLING
- Pictograms I

Level 3

NUMBERS
- **99999** 5-Digit Numbers
- **+/− 1234** Addition & Subtraction IV
- **×1** Multiplication I
- **2/24** Division I
- **+/− ×÷** Mixed Operations I
- **½** Fractions I

MEASURES
- **🕐** Time III
- **24:00** Time IV
- **📏 km** Length & Distance IV
- **📐** Capacity

SHAPES AND SPACE
- Parallel & Perpendicular Lines
- Quadrilaterals II
- Angles II
- Triangles

DATA HANDLING
- Block Graphs
- Bar Charts I

Level 4

NUMBERS
- **×12** Multiplication II
- **12)24** Division II
- **🖩** Calculators
- **1.2.4 1.2** Multiples & Factors
- **0/2.4 0/2** Common Multiples & Common Factors
- **+− ×÷** Mixed Operations II
- **2½** Fractions II
- **0.1** Decimals

MEASURES
- **▣** Perimeter I
- **▦** Area I

SHAPES AND SPACE
- Quadrilaterals III
- Fitting & Dissecting Shapes
- Simple Symmetry

DATA HANDLING
- Pictograms II

Numbers Are Everywhere!

Practice counting when you are in the neighborhood – count squirrels, blue houses, steps to the library, and so on. Count backwards as you travel to your destination or while you wait in a restaurant with your child.

What Is that Number?

Choose a number and offer clues about your chosen number, such as "This number comes before 8 and after 6." or "This number represents the number of days in one whole week." or "This number has two straight lines and begins with the letter s." See how quickly your child can guess the number, then allow him or her to give clues for you to guess.

Adding & Subtracting with Action

Give your child an equation and have him or her hop on one foot the correct number of times to show the answer. For example, "What is 3+3?" Your child would hop 6 times.

Or, use sidewalk chalk to write various two-digit numbers on the pavement, then give your child an addition or subtraction problem. See how quickly he or she can run, slide, hop, skate, spin, leap, or dance to the correct number to show the answer.

Shapes, Straight Lines & Curved Lines

Get creative with straight lines, curved lines, and shapes! Find two players (or more) sheets of paper, and different colored pens, markers, or crayons for each player. Each player should draw a line, shape, or squiggle on his or her sheet of paper. Trade papers, identify the lines and shapes you see, then add more lines and shapes to complete your picture. Play again!

Measure Me

Estimate, then help your child measure his or her height in feet and inches. Record your observation and measure again in a few months. Measure the distance from your child's elbow to shoulder, or from his or her knee to a big toe.

Longer/Shorter

Choose two household items (the couch and a bed) and ask your child – "Which is longer? Which is shorter?" After guessing, allow your child to measure the actual length (or height) of the two items to find the answer.

Numbers

10　**20**　**+/−**

1
LEVEL 1

This NUMBERS section introduces students to counting, reading, and writing numbers from 1 to 10 and 1 to 20. Students will also learn about ordinal numbers, odds & evens, counting backwards, adding numbers, subtracting, and more!

NUMBERS to 10
- Count, Read, and Write Numbers 1-10
- Counting On and Counting Backwards
- Even and Odd Numbers
- Comparing Groups of Objects
- Adding Groups of Objects Together

NUMBERS to 20
- Numbers 11 - 20
- Arranging the Numbers in Order
- Ordinal Numbers
- Adding Numbers Together

Basic Addition and Subtraction
- Putting Together and Taking Away Objects
- Adding and Subtracting (up to 18)
- The Number Zero
- Addition and Subtraction: Working Together
- Changing the Order in Addition (Commutative Property)

Counting

Learn It!

Numbers from 1 to 10.

1	2	3	4	5	6	7	8	9	10
one	two	three	four	five	six	seven	eight	nine	ten

← smaller   larger →

Numbers are used to count.
Count the oranges.

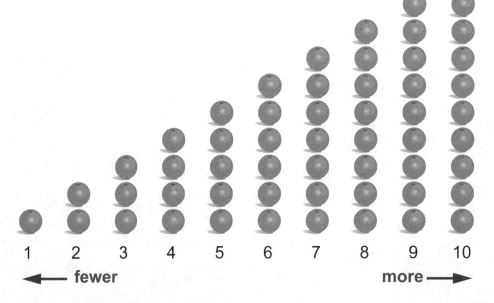

1   2   3   4   5   6   7   8   9   10

← fewer   more →

1, 3, 5, 7, and 9 are called **odd** numbers.
2, 4, 6, 8, and 10 are called **even** numbers.

1	2	3	4	5	6	7	8	9	10

Use It!

How many flowers are there?

count: 1   2   3   4   5   6   7   8

....

Count the number of flowers.
There are 8 flowers.

Answer

Which is **smaller**: 4 or 6?
(HINT: Count how many in each group of fruit.)

....

There are 4 mangoes and 6 apples.
There are fewer mangoes than apples.
The number 4 is smaller than 6.

Answer

Count, Read, and Write Numbers 1-10

Match the number to the set with the same number of objects.

4 •   • ★ ★ ★ ★ ★ ★ ★ ★

8 •   • ⬠ ⬠ ⬠

1 •   • ◣ ◣ ◣ ◣ ◣ ◣ ◣

3 •   • 🌙 🌙 🌙 🌙 🌙 🌙 🌙 🌙

6 •   • ● ●

5 •   • ▬

9 •   • ■ ■ ■ ■

2 •   • ▲ ▲ ▲ ▲ ▲ ▲

7 •   • ⬡ ⬡ ⬡ ⬡ ⬡ ⬡ ⬡ ⬡ ⬡ ⬡

10 •   • ▱ ▱ ▱ ▱ ▱

Trace and write the numbers 1 - 10 in number and word form.

1		one	one	
2		two	two	
3		three	three	
4		four	four	
5		five	five	
6		six	six	
7		seven	seven	
8		eight	eight	
9		nine	nine	
10		ten	ten	

Counting and Writing Numbers (i)

Count and write how many in number and word form.

Numbers to 10

Counting and Writing Numbers (ii)

10

Count and write how many in number form and word form.

 ★★★★★★	6	six
 (5 moons)		
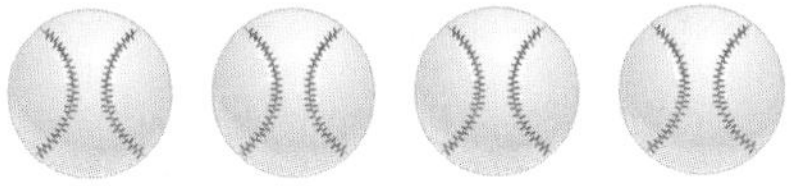 (4 baseballs)		
 (3 footballs)		
 (8 triangles)		
 (2 soccer balls)		
 (9 berries)		

Numbers to 10 11

Counting and Writing Numbers (iii)

Count and write how many in number and word form.

(4 elephants)	4	four
(6 dogs)		
(5 lions)		
(8 fish)		
(9 ducks)		
(7 rabbits)		

Count and write how many of each item.

_____ apples _____ oranges

_____ glasses of milk

_____ cans of soda

_____ shirts _____ dress

Count and write how many of each item.

_____ trees _____ flowers

_____ dogs _____ cats

_____ boy _____ girl

Fill in the missing numbers.

1,   _____,   3,   4

3,   4,   _____,   6

5,   _____,   7,   8

6,   7,   _____,   9

7,   8,   _____,   10

9,   8,   _____,   6

7,   _____,   5,   4

6,   5,   _____,   3

5,   4,   _____,   2

4,   _____,   2,   1

Counting on and Counting Backwards (ii)

Fill in the missing numbers.

| 1 | | 3 | 4 | | 6 | | 8 | | 10 |

| 10 | | 8 | 7 | | | 4 | 3 | | 1 |

| 1 | 2 | | 4 | 5 | | 7 | | | 10 |

| 10 | | | 7 | 6 | | 4 | | 2 | 1 |

| | 2 | 3 | | | 6 | 7 | | 9 | 10 |

| | 9 | | 7 | 6 | | 4 | 3 | 2 | |

Numbers to 10

Look at the counting sequence in each row. In the last box, draw the correct number of objects to complete each sequence.

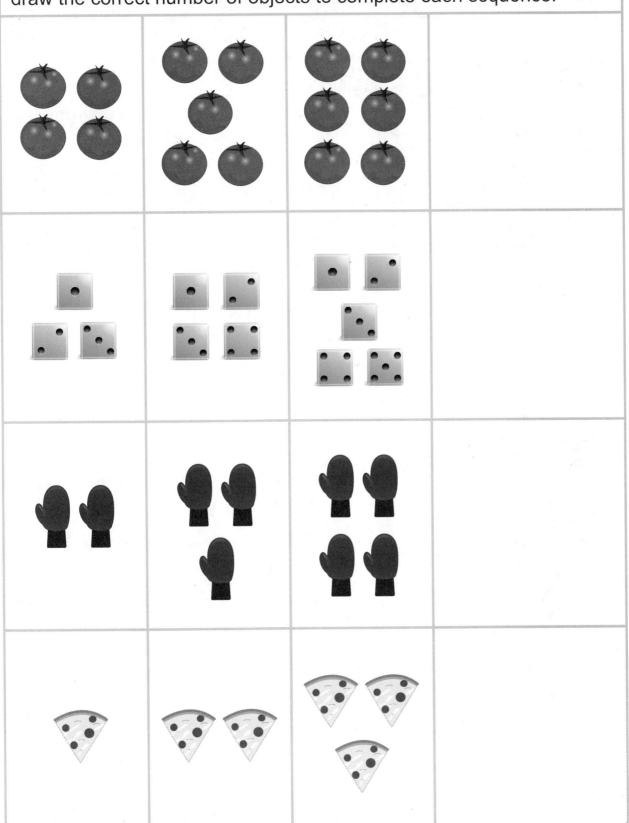

Counting on (ii)

Look at the counting sequence in each row. In the empty box, draw the correct number of objects to complete each sequence.

Numbers to 10

Circle the **even** number in each row.
Even numbers can be found by skip-counting from number 2.

1,   2,   3,   5,   7

3,   4,   5,   7,   9

3,   5,   6,   7,   9

3,   5,   7,   8,   9

3,   5,   7,   9,   10

1,   3,   5,   7,   8

3
4
5
6
7
8
9
8
7
6
5
4
3

Even and Odd Numbers (ii)

Circle the **odd** number in each row.
Odd numbers can be found by skip-counting from number 1.

2,   3,   6,   8,   10

1,   2,   4,   6,   8

2,   4,   6,   7,   10

2,   4,   5,   6,   8

2,   3,   4,   6,   8

4,   6,   8,   9,   10

4,   6,   7,   8,   10

Numbers to 10

Circle the **even** numbers. Draw a box around the **odd** numbers.

7

2

8

5

9   3   4

6

1   10

6

10

5

9

4

2   8

3   7

1

How many **odd** numbers in all? _____

How many **even** numbers in all? _____

Even and Odd Numbers (iv)

Fill in the other **even** numbers.

| 2 | | 6 | | 10 |

Fill in the other **odd** numbers.

| 1 | | 5 | | 9 |

Fill in the missing **even** numbers.

| 1 | | 3 | | 5 | | 7 | | 9 |

Fill in the missing **odd** numbers.

| 2 | | 4 | | 6 | | 8 | | 10 |

Numbers to 10

Comparing Groups of Objects (i)

Count. Circle the group with **fewer** objects.

 or

 or

 or

 or

Comparing Groups of Objects (ii)

Count. Circle the group with **more** objects.

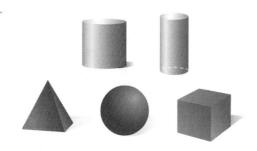 or

 or

 or

 or

Numbers to 10

Count and write how many in each box.

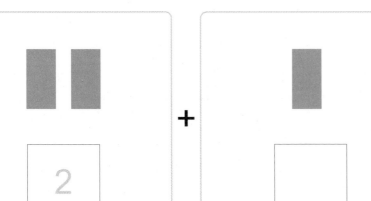

Draw the total number of orange blocks.

Write how many orange blocks in all.

Two plus one equals _____.

2   +   1   =   _____.

3 4 5 6 7 8 9 8 7 6 5 4 3

Adding Groups of Objects Together (ii)

Count and write how many in each box.

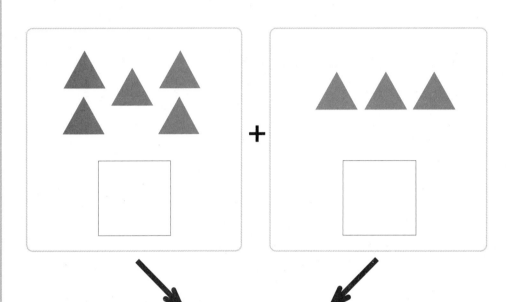

Draw the total number of green triangles.

Write how many green triangles in all.

Five plus three equals _____.

5   +   3   =   _____.

How many objects are missing? Draw the objects that are missing to make the groups equal. Write the number to show how many objects you added to make the groups equal.

 =

_____ footballs were missing.

 =

_____ leaves were missing.

 =

_____ markers were missing.

Adding Numbers Together (i)

Write the correct number on the line to finish each sentence.

| 1 | 2 | 3 | 4 | 5 | 6 | 7 | 8 | 9 | 10 |

9 plus 1 more equals _____.

3 plus 2 more equals _____.

5 plus 4 more equals _____.

3 plus 6 more equals _____.

2 plus 7 more equals _____.

5 plus 4 more equals _____.

6 plus 3 more equals _____.

8 plus 2 more equals _____.

Numbers to 10

Write the correct number on the line to finish each sentence.

| 1 | 2 | 3 | 4 | 5 | 6 | 7 | 8 | 9 | 10 |

3 plus 1 equals _____.

5 plus 4 equals _____.

9 plus 1 equals _____.

6 plus 2 equals _____.

2 plus 3 equals _____.

1 plus 4 equals _____.

7 plus 2 equals _____.

5 plus 1 equals _____.

⭐ Star Question

Use this diagram to answer the questions on the next page.

There are _____ lemons.

There are _____ fish.

There are _____ flowers.

Is there an **even** or an **odd** number of frogs?

_____

Is there an **even** or an **odd** number of

bananas?_____

The number of frogs and the number of fish

make _____ animals in all.

_____ frogs + _____ fish = _____ animals

Counting

Learn It!

Numbers from 11 - 20.

11 eleven	→	12 twelve	→	13 thirteen	→	14 fourteen	→	15 fifteen
16 sixteen	→	17 seventeen	→	18 eighteen	→	19 nineteen	→	20 twenty

Numbers in blue are **odd** numbers.
Numbers in green are **even** numbers.

Numbers are used in counting. Count the ducks.

There are 10 ducks in the top row.
There are 6 ducks in the bottom row.
There are 16 ducks in all.

Numbers can also be used to count things in order.
These are **ordinal** numbers.

1st 2nd 3rd 4th 5th 6th

first second third fourth fifth sixth

Use It!

How many penguins are there?

....

There are 10 penguins in the top row, and 3 penguins in the bottom row. So, there are 13 penguins in all.

Answer

What color is the third dog from the left?
(HINT: "Third" is the same as "3.ʳᵈ")

....

The third dog is green.

Answer

Count, Read, and Write Numbers 11-20

Trace and write the numbers and words from 11-20.

11		eleven	eleven	
12		twelve	twelve	
13		thirteen	thirteen	
14		fourteen	fourteen	
15		fifteen	fifteen	
16		sixteen	sixteen	
17		seventeen	seventeen	
18		eighteen	eighteen	
19		nineteen	nineteen	
20		twenty	twenty	

Numbers to 20

Match the number to the word.

11 •   • fourteen

12 •   • twenty

13 •   • twelve

14 •   • nineteen

15 •   • eleven

16 •   • eighteen

17 •   • sixteen

18 •   • fifteen

19 •   • thirteen

20 •   • seventeen

Number Words (ii)

Write the numbers in words.

1 _____   2 _____

3 _____   4 _____

5 _____   6 _____

7 _____   8 _____

9 _____   10 _____

16 _____   17 _____

18 _____   19 _____

20 _____   15 _____

12 _____   11 _____

14 _____   13 _____

Numbers to 20

Count the objects. Write how many in number and word form.

_____

_____

_____

_____

_____

_____

_____

_____

_____

_____

3
4
5
6
7
8
9
8
7
6
5
4
3

Number Words (iv)

Count the objects. Write how many in number and word form.

_____

_____

_____

_____

_____

_____

_____

_____

_____

_____

Numbers to 20

Arranging the Numbers in Order (i)

Arrange the numbers from **lowest** to **highest**.
Some numbers are missing.

 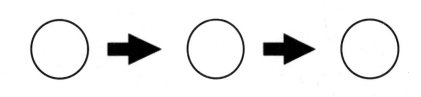

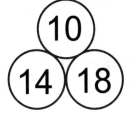 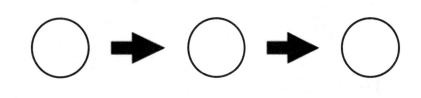

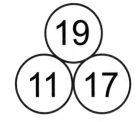 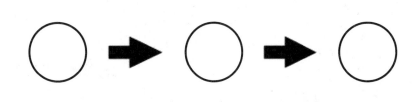

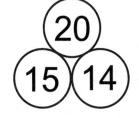 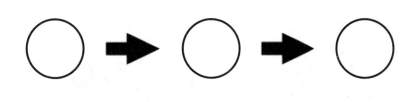

Arranging the Numbers in Order (ii)

Arrange the numbers from **lowest** to **highest**.
Some numbers may be missing.

 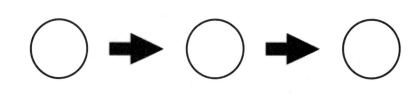

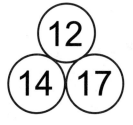 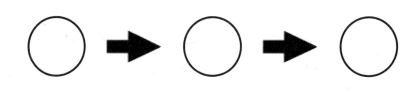

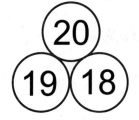 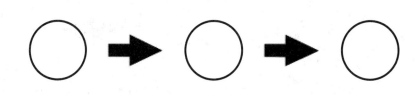

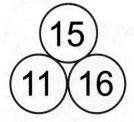 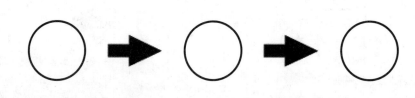

Numbers to 20

Fill in the missing numbers.

11, ___, 13, 14, 15, 16

15, 16, ___, 18, 19, 20

12, 13, 14, ___, 16, 17

10, 11, 12, 13, ___, 15

20, 19, ___, 17, 16, 15

18, 17, 16, 15, 14, ___

15, ___, 13, 12, 11, 10

17, 16, 15, ___, 13, 12

___, 15, 14, 13, 12, 11

Ordinal Numbers (i)

Practice writing **ordinal** numbers.

1st		first	first
2nd		second	second
3rd		third	third
4th		fourth	fourth
5th		fifth	fifth
6th		sixth	sixth
7th		seventh	seventh
8th		eighth	eighth
9th		ninth	ninth
10th		tenth	tenth

Numbers to 20

Match the number to the word.

1st •   • fifth

2nd •   • seventh

3rd •   • fourth

4th •   • second

5th •   • sixth

6th •   • first

7th •   • eighth

8th •   • tenth

9th •   • third

10th •   • ninth

Ordinal Numbers (iii)

Circle the object that is in the 2nd place.

| 1st | 2nd | 3rd | 4th | 5th |

Circle the object that is in the 3rd place.

Circle the object that is in the 4th place.

Numbers to 20

Count and write how many in each box.
Draw the total number of objects in the last box.

 + 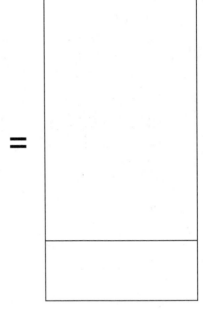 =

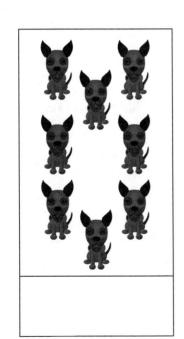 +  =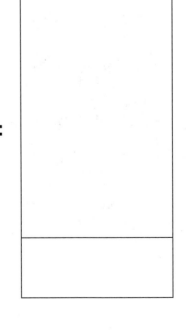

Adding Numbers Together (ii)

Count and write how many in each box.
Draw the total number of objects in the last box.

 +  =

 +  =

Numbers to 20

Write the correct number on the line to finish each sentence.

13 plus 5 equals _____.

15 plus 1 equals _____.

9 plus 8 equals _____.

13 plus 2 equals _____.

9 plus 3 equals _____.

11 plus 6 equals _____.

7 plus 7 equals _____.

10 plus 3 equals _____.

12 plus 6 equals _____.

10 plus 2 equals _____.

Review (i)

Count the objects and write how many.

_____ fish

_____bunches
of grapes

_____ glasses

Write the number as a word.

14 _____

15 _____

17 _____

19 _____

Numbers to 20

Add and write the correct number on the line to finish each sentence.

13 plus 5 equals _____.

15 plus 1 equals _____.

9 plus 8 equals _____.

Match the number to the word.

6 •   • second

8th •   • eighth

15 •   • seventh

7th •   • six

2nd •   • fifteen

★ Star Question

Solve.

Mary has 8 stickers.
Jeannie has 5 stickers.
Johnny has 11 stickers.

How many stickers do Mary
and Jeannie have in all? _____

How many **more** stickers
does Johnny have than Mary? _____

How many **more** stickers does
Johnny have than Jeannie? _____

How many stickers do the
three of them have in all? _____

Learn It!

Addition means putting two groups together.
Add 3 cats and 2 cats.
There are 5 cats in all.

Addition

Subtraction

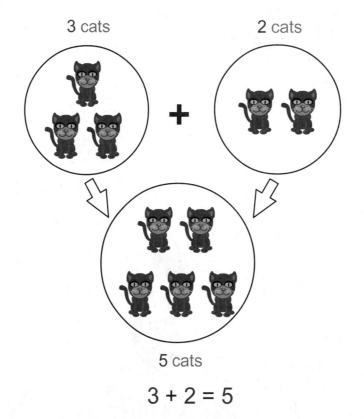

3 cats   2 cats

5 cats

$$3 + 2 = 5$$

Subtraction means taking things away.
Subtract 2 dogs from 4 dogs.
There are 2 dogs left.

$$4 - 2 = 2$$

(4 minus 2 equals 2)

Use It!

There are two koalas. Add 1 more koala. How many in all?

....

Count the number of koalas.
There are 3 koalas in all. (2 + 1 = 3).

Answer

There are 4 pies. Subtract the two pies that have been eaten. How many pies are left?

....

Take away 2 pies from 4 pies.
There are 2 pies left (4 - 2 = 2).

Answer

Amanda has 5 flowers.
Caroline has 2 flowers.

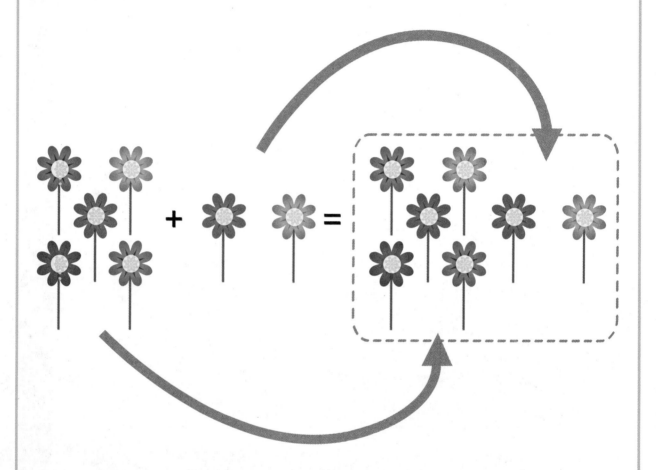

How many flowers do they have in all?

_____

Sam has 6 toy cars.
Jim has 8 toy cars.

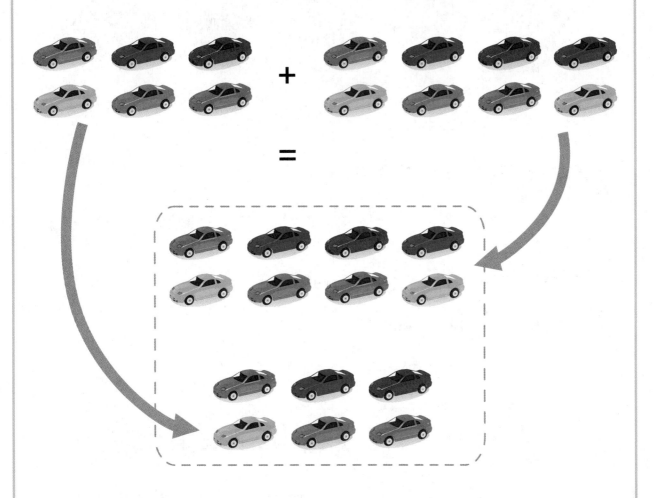

How many toy cars do they have in all?

_____

There were 5 shirts in Joe's closet.
He gave away 2 shirts.

How many shirts are left?   _____

Kathy had 15 peaches.
She ate 8 peaches.

How many peaches are left?   _____

Write the numbers to help solve the picture equations.

  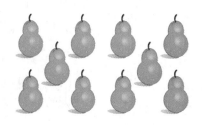

\+ _____ = _____

_____   +   _____   =   _____

_____   +   _____   =   _____

_____   +   _____   =   _____

3 4 5 6 7 8 9 8 7 6 5 4 3

Write the numbers to help solve the picture equations.

_____ - _____ = _____

_____ - _____ = _____

_____ - _____ = _____

Basic Addition and Subtraction

+/−

Draw pictures to show each number sentence.

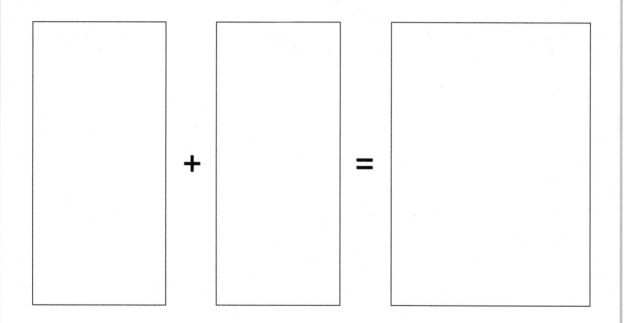

6 flowers + 5 flowers = _____ flowers

4 squares + 5 squares = _____ squares

3 4 5 6 7 8 9 8 7 6 5 4 3

Draw pictures to show each number sentence.

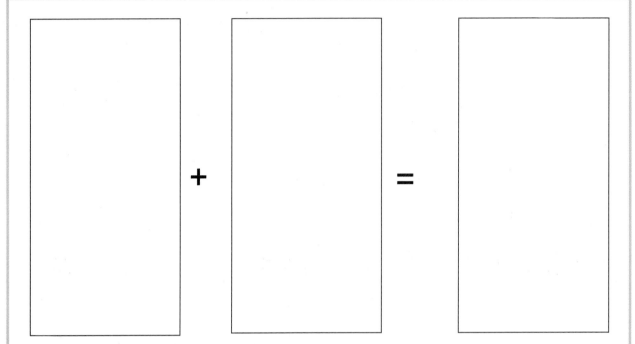

7 baseballs + 3 baseballs = _____baseballs

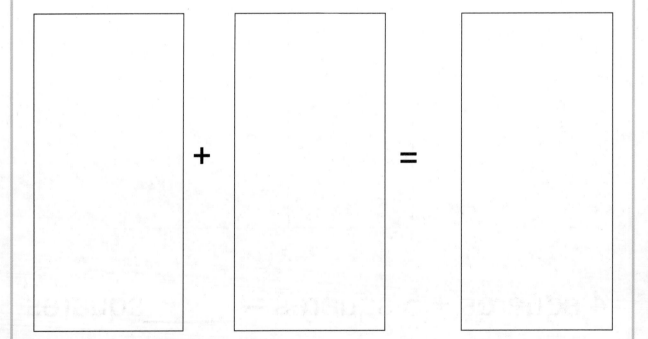

6 dogs + 2 dogs = _____ dogs

+/−

Add.

1 + 1 = ___   2 + 2 = ___   3 + 3 = ___

1 + 2 = ___   2 + 3 = ___   3 + 4 = ___

1 + 3 = ___   2 + 4 = ___   3 + 5 = ___

1 + 4 = ___   2 + 5 = ___   3 + 6 = ___

1 + 5 = ___   2 + 6 = ___   3 + 7 = ___

1 + 6 = ___   2 + 7 = ___   3 + 8 = ___

1 + 7 = ___   2 + 8 = ___   3 + 9 = ___

1 + 8 = ___   2 + 9 = ___   3 + 10 = ___

1 + 9 = ___   2 + 10 = ___

1 + 10 = ___

3 4 5 6 7 8 9 8 7 6 5 4 3

Add.

$5 + 5 =$ ___ $6 + 6 =$ ___ $7 + 7 =$ ___

$5 + 6 =$ ___ $6 + 7 =$ ___ $7 + 8 =$ ___

$5 + 7 =$ ___ $6 + 8 =$ ___ $7 + 9 =$ ___

$5 + 8 =$ ___ $6 + 9 =$ ___ $7 + 10 =$ ___

$5 + 9 =$ ___ $6 + 10 =$ ___

$5 + 10 =$ ___

$8 + 8 =$ ___ $9 + 9 =$ ___

$8 + 9 =$ ___ $9 + 10 =$ ___

$8 + 10 =$ ___

Basic Addition and Subtraction

Write the correct number on the line to show the **difference** between the groups of objects.

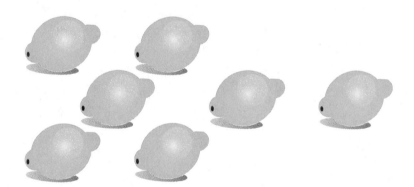

There are 12 apples and 7 lemons.

12 - 7 = _____

There are _____ **more** apples than there are lemons.

Write the correct number on the line to show the **difference** between the groups of objects.

There are 9 spoons and 6 forks.

9 - 6 = _____

There are _____ **more** spoons than there are forks.

+/-

Subtract.

12 - 2 = _____   12 - 1 = _____

12 - 4 = _____   12 - 3 = _____

12 - 6 = _____   12 - 5 = _____

12 - 8 = _____   12 - 7 = _____

12 - 10 = _____   12 - 9 = _____

16 - 3 = _____   12 - 11 = _____

16 - 6 = _____   16 - 4 = _____

16 - 9 = _____   16 - 8 = _____

16 - 2 = _____   16 - 12 = _____

Subtracting (iv)

Subtract.

18 - 1 = _____   18 - 11 = _____

18 - 2 = _____   18 - 12 = _____

18 - 3 = _____   18 - 13 = _____

18 - 4 = _____   18 - 14 = _____

18 - 5 = _____   18 - 15 = _____

18 - 6 = _____   18 - 16 = _____

18 - 7 = _____   18 - 17 = _____

18 - 8 = _____

18 - 9 = _____

18 - 10 = _____

Basic Addition and Subtraction

Adding up to 18

Add.

5 + 3 = _____   12 + 3 = _____

2 + 6 = _____   9 + 5 = _____

3 + 8 = _____   6 + 7 = _____

7 + 9 = _____   6 + 8 = _____

4 + 8 = _____   5 + 7 = _____

5 + 6 = _____   4 + 6 = _____

12 + 4 = _____   3 + 9 = _____

10 + 5 = _____   11 + 5 = _____

13 + 4 = _____   13 + 4 = _____

11 + 6 = _____   10 + 8 = _____

15 + 1 = _____   9 + 7 = _____

Basic Addition and Subtraction

67

Subtract.

15 - 4 = _____   14 - 7 = _____

12 - 8 = _____   15 - 9 = _____

14 - 3 = _____   18 - 3 = _____

10 - 6 = _____   16 - 2 = _____

13 - 7 = _____   17 - 2 = _____

12 - 5 = _____   11 - 3 = _____

8 - 4 = _____   10 - 7 = _____

14 - 8 = _____   13 - 6 = _____

9 - 4 = _____   17 - 4 = _____

6 - 2 = _____   11 - 8 = _____

12 - 3 = _____   13 - 5 = _____

Pick a number from the bubble to complete each number sentence.

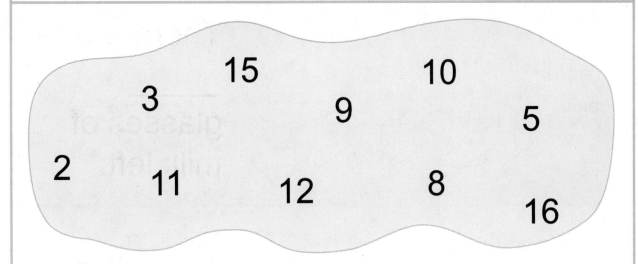

11 - 3 = _____

15 - 3 = _____

10 + _____ = 12

_____ + 4 = 9

8 + 7 = _____

8 + 2 = _____

14 - 3 = _____

18 - 15 = _____

7 + _____ = 16

4 + 12 = _____

The Number Zero (i)

How many are left?

before:

after:

There are

_____

glasses of milk left.

before:

after:

There are

_____

cookies left.

before:

after:

There are

_____

cakes left.

before:

after:

There are

_____

grapes left.

Basic Addition and Subtraction

A number plus or minus 0 equals the number.
Add. Adding 0 is like adding nothing.

$18 + 0 =$ _____

$0 + 6 =$ _____

$4 + 0 =$ _____

$0 + 3 =$ _____

$9 + 0 =$ _____

$0 + 15 =$ _____

$13 + 0 =$ _____

$0 + 10 =$ _____

A number minus that same number equals 0.
Subtract. Subtracting 0 is like subtracting nothing.

$14 - 0 =$ _____

$14 - 14 =$ _____

$5 - 5 =$ _____

$5 - 0 =$ _____

$7 - 7 =$ _____

$7 - 0 =$ _____

$16 - 16 =$ _____

$16 - 0 =$ _____

Addition and Subtraction: Working Together (i)

Write how many below the pictures.

_____ cupcakes + _____ cupcakes = _____ cupcakes

_____ cupcakes in all - _____ cupcakes = _____ cupcakes

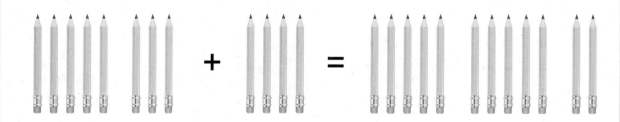

_____ pencils + _____ pencils = _____ pencils

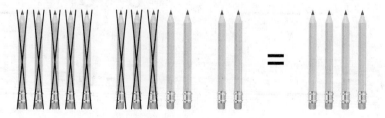

_____ pencils in all - _____ pencils = _____ pencils

Basic Addition and Subtraction

Write how many below the pictures.

_____ apples + _____ apples = _____ apples

_____ apples in all - _____ apples = _____ apples

_____ apples + _____ apples = _____ apples

_____ apples in all - _____ apples = _____ apples

Pick a number from the bubble to complete each number sentence.

10 + _____ = 14 and 14 - 4 = _____

6 + 3 = _____ and 9 - _____ = 6

5 + _____ = 12 and _____ - 7 = 5

_____ + 2 = 15 and _____ - 2 = 13

Basic Addition and Subtraction

Changing the Order in Addition (Commutative Property) (i)

Write the missing numbers below the pictures.

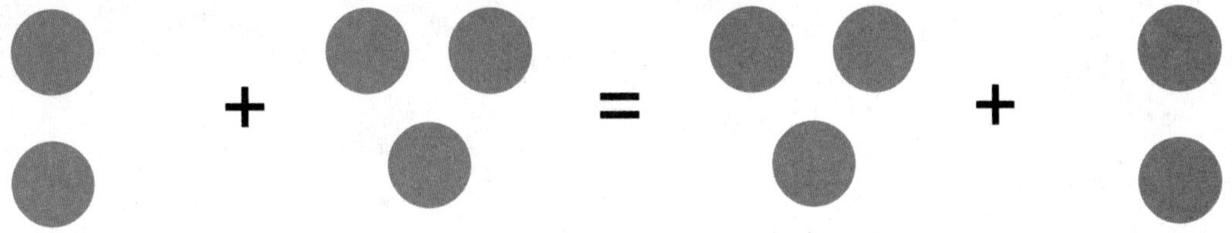

________ + ________ = ________ + ________

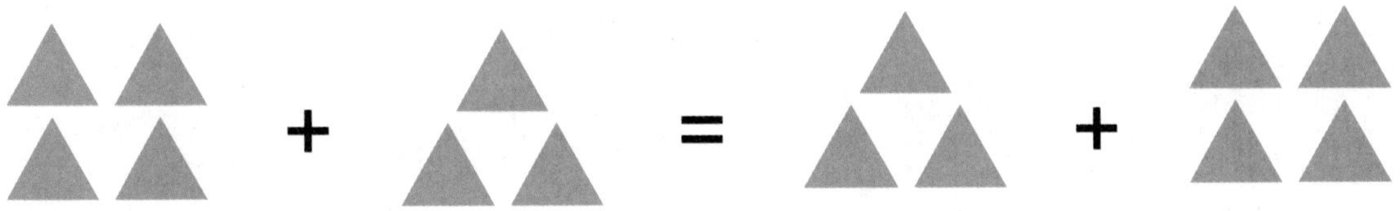

________ + ________ = ________ + ________

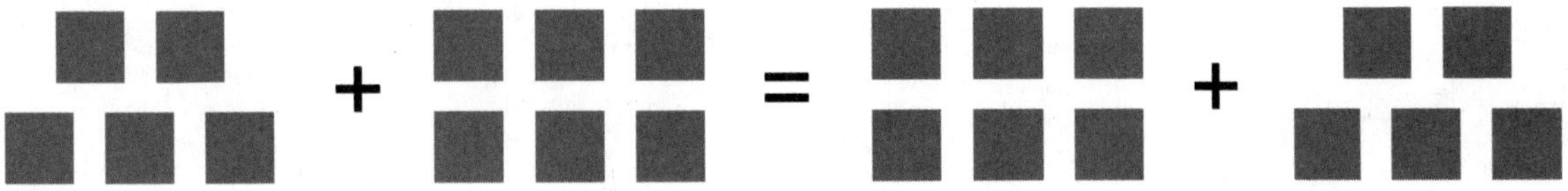

________ + ________ = ________ + ________

Write the missing numbers and draw the missing pictures.

 **+** ☐ **=**  **+** ☐

_____   _____   _____   _____

☐ **+** ✩✩✩✩ **=** ☐ **+** ✩✩✩✩✩✩✩✩✩

_____   _____   _____   _____

🌙🌙🌙🌙🌙🌙🌙🌙 **+** ☐ **=** 🌙🌙🌙🌙🌙 **+** ☐

_____   _____   _____   _____

+/−

Add to find how many hearts in all.

_____ hearts +   _____ hearts =   _____ hearts in all.

Count and write the number to show how many pairs of pants in all.
Cross out 3 pairs of pants. Count how many are left and write the answer.

_____ pairs of pants in all - 3 pairs of pants = _____ pairs of pants

---

Add.

$$13 + 5 = \text{\_\_\_\_\_}$$ $$9 + 7 = \text{\_\_\_\_\_}$$

$$6 + 4 = \text{\_\_\_\_\_}$$ $$8 + 6 = \text{\_\_\_\_\_}$$

$$7 + 6 = \text{\_\_\_\_\_}$$ $$14 + 3 = \text{\_\_\_\_\_}$$

Star Question

Solve.

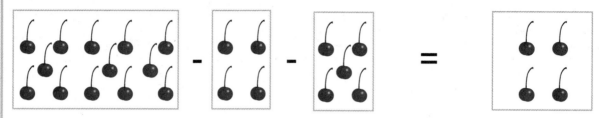

13   -   4   -   5   =   _____

Part 1 Answer

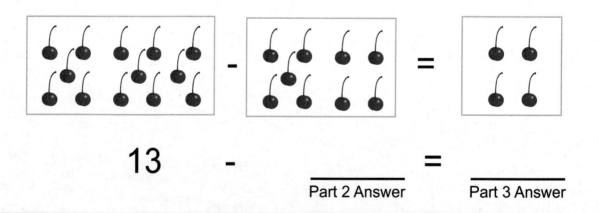

4   +   5   =   _____

Part 2 Answer

13   -   _____   =   _____

Part 2 Answer   Part 3 Answer

What is interesting about the answers from Part 1 and Part 3?

_____

Basic Addition and Subtraction

Numbers Tools - Number Cards

Directions: Cut out the number cards on the black lines.

Try these ideas or make up your own ways to play with the number cards:

1. Practice putting numbers in order from lowest to highest.
2. Place all the even numbered cards in one pile and all the odd numbers in another.
3. Use the cards to practice skip-counting by 2, 5, or 10.
4. Place the cards in reverse order from 20 to 1.
5. Use the cards to build and solve your own addition or subtraction equations.

1	2	3	4	5
6	7	8	9	10
11	12	13	14	15
16	17	18	19	20

Numbers Tools - Number Cards

More Ideas:

1. Place all the number cards in a pile. Pick a card. See how quickly you can find that number in your home. Race a friend!

2. Pick a number. How many things can you name that relate to that number - for example: 3 little pigs, 8 sides on a stop sign, 12 eggs in a dozen, and so on.

3. Shuffle the cards and deal them into two piles. Find a friend to play and take turns placing a card on the table. The player with the highest number gets to keep both cards. Continue play until all the cards have been won.

-	+	=	-	+
11	**12**	**13**	**14**	**15**
6	**7**	**8**	**9**	**10**
1	**2**	**3**	**4**	**5**

Numbers Tools - Picture Cards

+/−
12

Directions: Cut out the cards on the black lines. Then, try these ideas or think of your own:

1. Select all the cards that have the same picture (e.g. stars). Place them on the table and count to find how many stars in all. Flip the cards over and count again.
2. Use the +, -, and = symbols to create your own picture equations. For example, you might place the following cards in order: 5 flowers + 2 flowers = 7 flowers.
3. Choose 2 cards with the same picture (e.g. fish). Which card shows more fish? Which card shows fewer fish? Can you find two cards that have the same number of objects?

Numbers Tools - Picture Cards

More Ideas:

1. Use the number cards and the picture cards to match groups of objects and the number that shows how many. For example, you might match the picture of 4 circles with the card that shows the number 4.

2. Create your own subtraction story problems with the cards. For example, you might say, "Megan had 6 flowers. She picked 3 flowers to give to her friend. How many does she have left?" Use the cards to show the equation and the answer 6 - 3 = 3.

3. Create a pattern with the cards (e.g. 2 stars, 4 stars, 6 stars, 8 stars). Encourage a friend to guess the pattern and create a pattern that is similar.

Numbers Tools

Numbers Tools - Subtraction Stories

Directions: Cut out the cards on the black lines. Then, try these ideas or think of your own:

Make up your own stories about the picture cards. For example, 5 ducks were walking near the pond. 2 ducks jumped in the water. How many ducks were left on land? Use the Number Cards to show the answer.

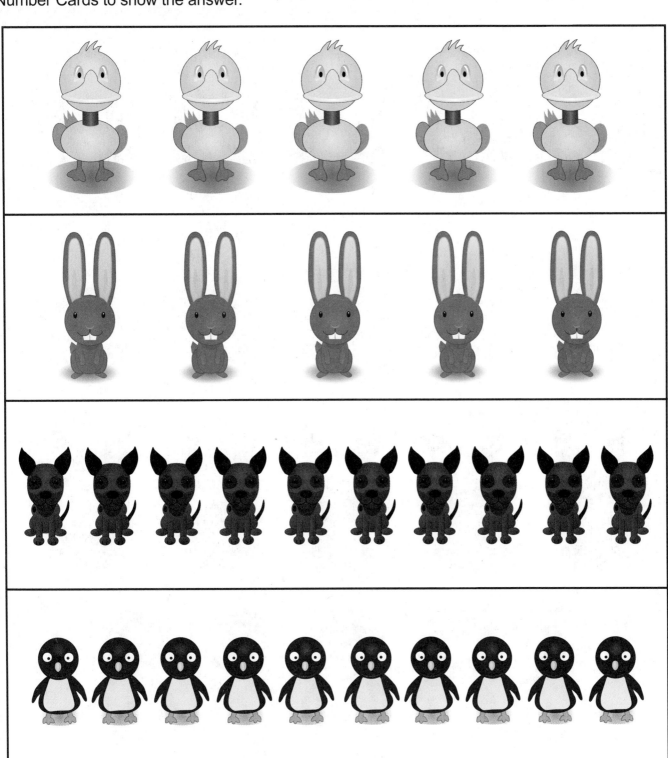

Numbers Tools - Subtraction Stories

More Ideas:

Use the cards to make up your own addition stories, too. For example, 5 dogs plus 5 penguins equals 10 animals in all.

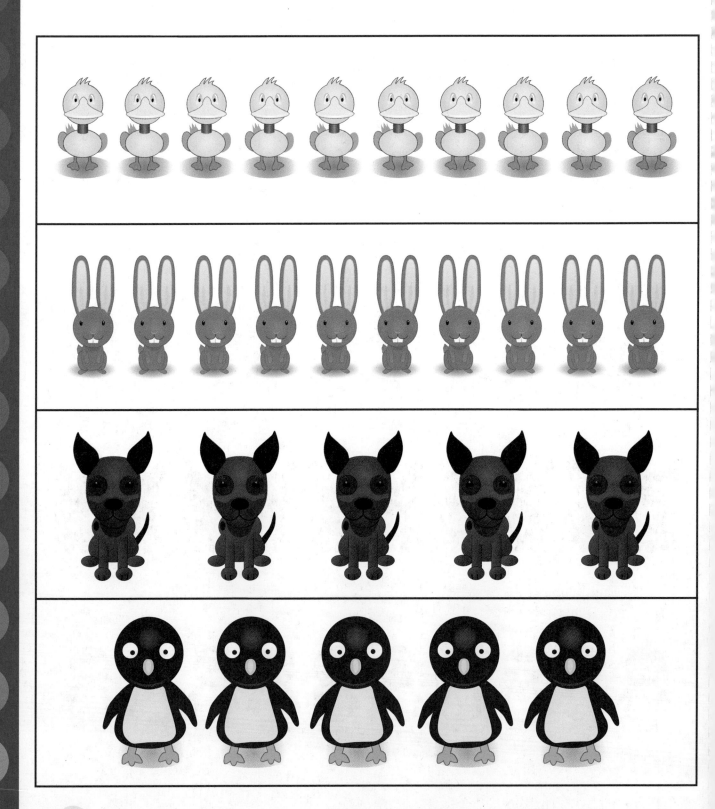

Numbers Tools - Subtraction Stories

More Ideas:

Use the cards to compare the groups of animals. Which cards show more animals? Which card shows fewer animals? What is the difference in the size of the groups?

Numbers Tools - Subtraction Stories

More Ideas:

Make your own Subtraction Story Cards. Draw your own pictures, use stickers, or cut pictures out of a magazine. Use your cards to make up your own picture word problems.

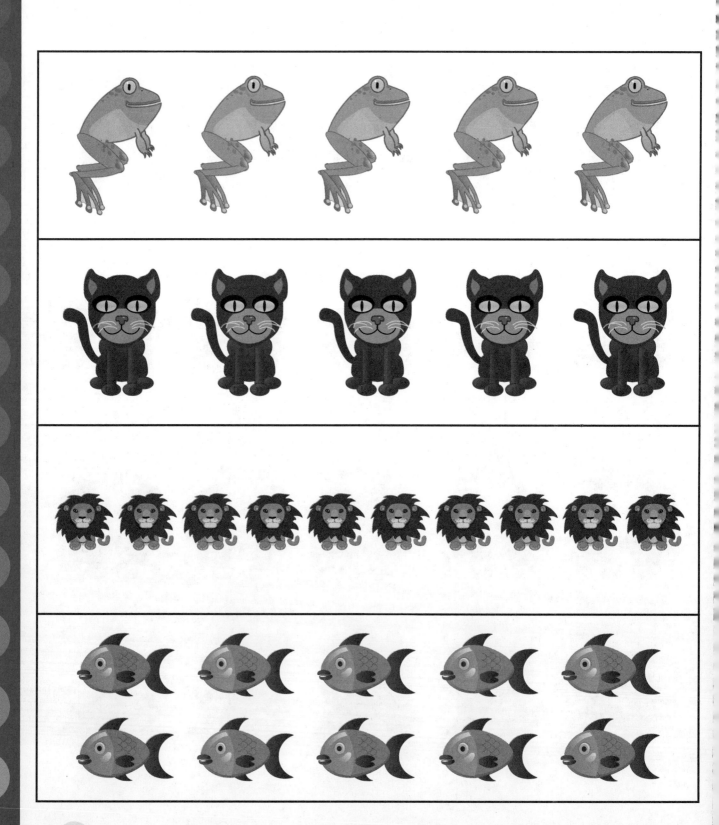

Congratulations!
Great Work!

Your Name

You have successfully completed the requirements for the workbook practice section of:

10 20 +/−

GRADE 1 LEVEL 1
NUMBERS

Professor Mugo

PLANETii Director of Learning

Please enter this code to gain six stars from your SmartMath Practice round. These stars will increase your iiPoints and assist you when you are ready to challenge for this topic at

www.britannicasmartmath.com/workbook

5429

Planetii Est.since 2000

login@

www.britannicasmartmath.com/workbook

username

password

=

Don't forget to claim your stars and iipoints online.

1 + 1 = You are
2 Awesome!

Measures

LEVEL 1

This MEASURES section introduces students to the concept of measuring with non-standard and standard units. Additionally, students will compare lengths and find the distance between objects.

LENGTH AND DISTANCE I

- Comparing Lengths of Objects
- Comparing Distances Between Objects
- Estimating Lengths with Everyday Items
- Why Do We Need a Ruler?
- Standard and Non-Standard Measures
- Using an Inch Ruler
- Identifying Length
- Distance Between Objects

Length and Distance I
LEVEL 1 MEASURES

Learn It!

The **distance** between two objects measures how far they are from each other.

The **length** of an object measures how **long** or how **short** it is.

Everyday objects, like paper clips can be used to estimate distance and length.

The **distance** between these two birds is 5 paper clips.

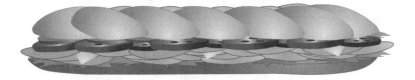

This sandwich is 4 paper clips long.

The stamp is 1 paper clip wide.

Use It!

Example 1

What is the distance between the bear and the rabbit?

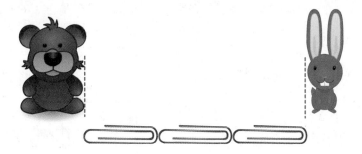

Answer:
The distance between the bear and the rabbit is 3 paper clips.

Answer

Example 2

How long is the fork? How long is the knife? How many paper clips longer is the knife than the fork?

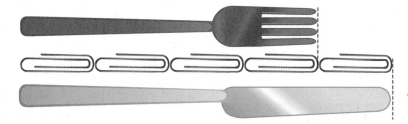

Answer:
The fork is 4 paper clips long. The knife is 5 paper clips long. The knife is 1 paper clip longer than the fork (5 paper clips - 4 paper clips = 1 paper clip).

Answer

Comparing Lengths of Objects (i)

Draw a ✔ next to the **longer** object.

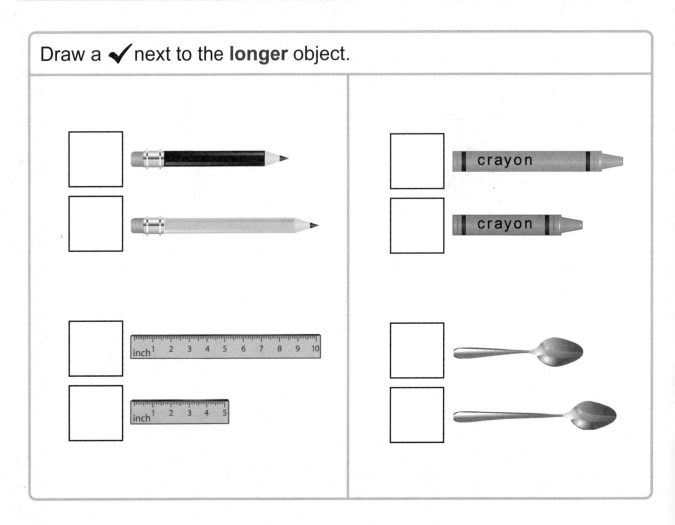

Draw a ✔ next to the **longest** object.

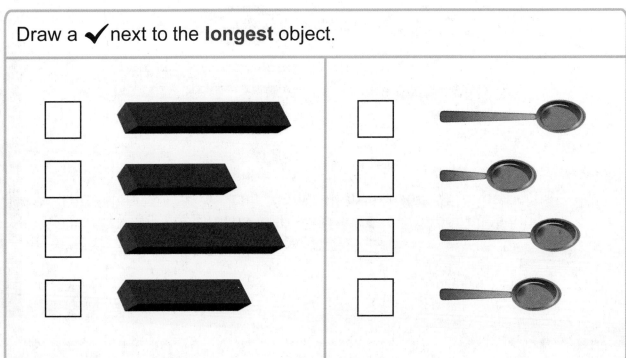

Length and Distance I

Comparing Lengths of Objects (ii)

Draw a ✔ next to the **shorter** object.

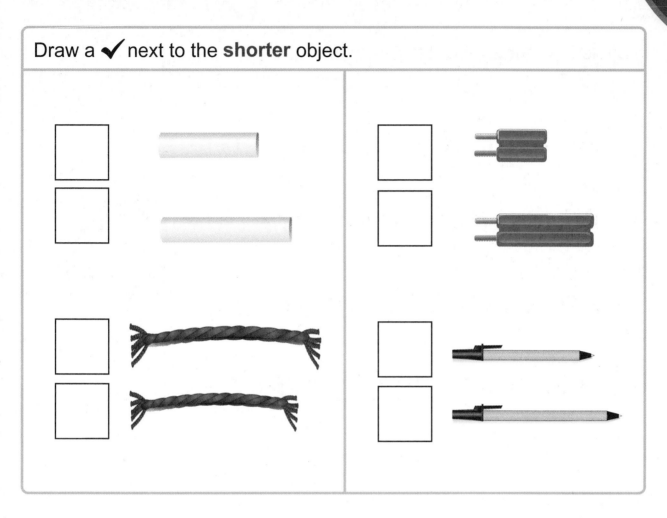

Draw a ✔ next to the **shortest** object.

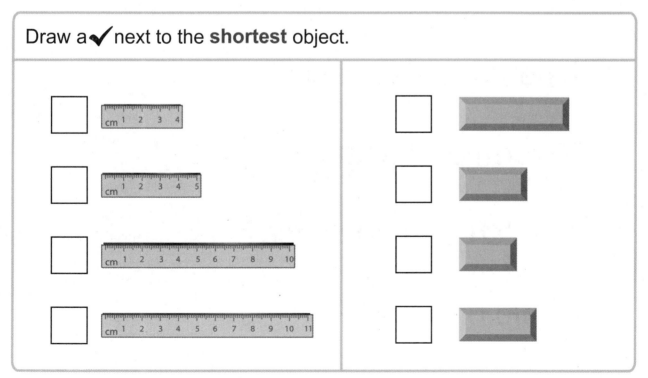

Circle the **longer** object in each pair.

An airplane or a bus?

A jump rope or a ruler?

An eraser or a comb?

A stamp or an envelope?

Which is **shorter**? Write your answer.

A pen or a paper clip?   _____

A worm or a snake?   _____

A watch or a necklace?   _____

A ship or a boat?   _____

Draw a ✔ below the **taller** object.

☐   ☐

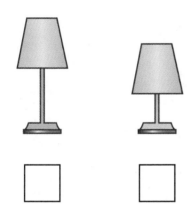

☐   ☐

☐   ☐

Draw a ✔ below the **tallest** object.

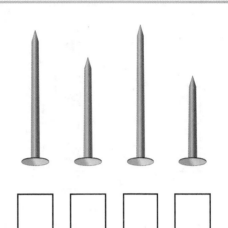

☐ ☐ ☐ ☐

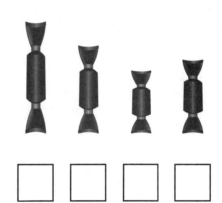

☐ ☐ ☐ ☐

☐ ☐ ☐ ☐

Comparing Heights of Objects (ii)

Draw a ✔ below the **shorter** object.

Draw a ✔ below the **shortest** object.

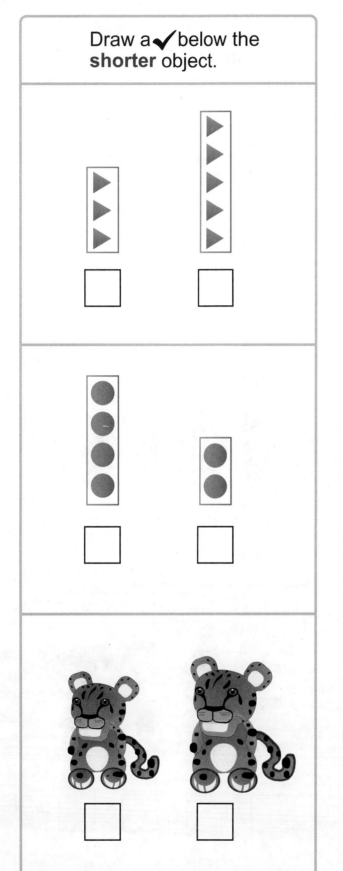

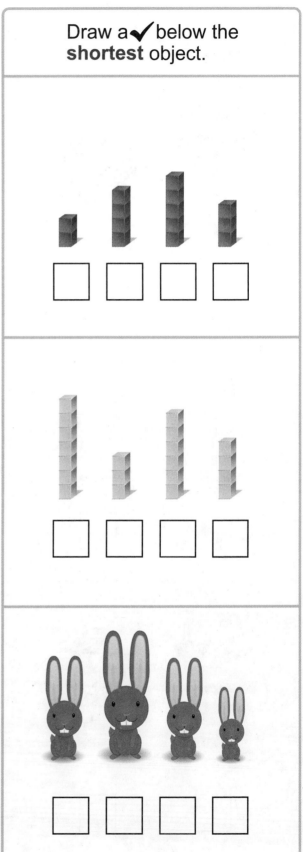

Length and Distance I

Which is **taller**? Write your answer.

A mountain or a bookshelf?   _____

A milk carton or a chair?   _____

A computer or a refrigerator?   _____

A baby or an adult?   _____

Which is **shorter**? Write your answer.

A lamp or a house?   _____

A flagpole or a candle?   _____

A soda can or a trash can?   _____

A giraffe or a dog?   _____

Use the diagram to answer the following questions.

—— A ——

———————————— B ————————————

———————————— C ————————————

Line B shows a **longer** distance than line _____.

Line _____ shows a **longer** distance than line B.

Which line shows the **longest** distance? _____

Use the diagram to answer the following questions.

———————————— A ———————————

——— B ———

——————————— C ———————————

Line A is **shorter** than Line _____.

Line _____ is **shorter** than Line A.

Which line shows the **shortest**

distance? _____

Comparing Distances Between Objects (iii)

Draw a ✔ next to the **longest** distance.

☐ Your head to your shoulders

OR

☐ Your head to your toes

☐ Your bedroom to your school

OR

☐ Your bedroom to your bathroom

☐ The distance between your eyes

OR

☐ The distance between your ears

☐ Your stomach to your knee

OR

☐ Your nose to your chin

Length and Distance I

How many paper clips **long** are the objects?

_____ paper clips

_____ paper clips

_____ paper clip

_____ paper clips

_____ paper clips

How many thumb tacks **tall** is each object?

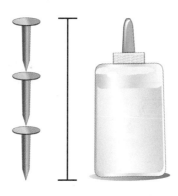

_____ thumb tacks

_____ thumb tacks

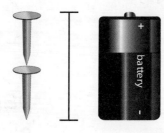

_____ thumb tacks

Length and Distance I

What is the distance between each pair of objects?
How many paper clips or blocks **long** is the distance?

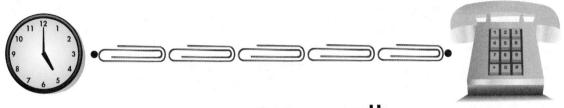

_____ paper clips

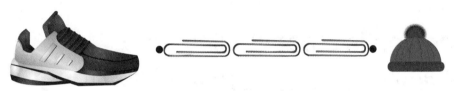

_____ paper clips

_____ blocks

_____ blocks

Complete each measurement with the correct number.

The crayon is 3 paper clips **long**.
The pencil is _____ paper clips **long**.

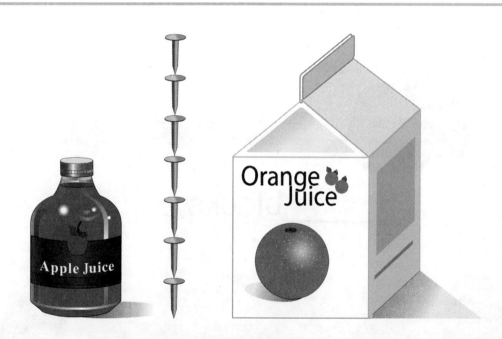

The bottle is 4 thumb tacks **tall**.
The juice carton is _____ thumb
tacks **tall**.

What is the total length of the two items added together?

A pencil is 7 blocks **long** and
a crayon is 4 blocks **long**.
Total length: _____ blocks

$$\begin{array}{r} 7 \\ + \ 4 \\ \hline \end{array}$$

A book is 6 blocks **long** and
a marker is 3 blocks **long**.
Total length: _____ blocks

$$\begin{array}{r} 6 \\ + \ 3 \\ \hline \end{array}$$

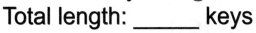

A cheese slice is 2 keys **long** and a
shoe is 4 keys **long**.
Total length: _____ keys

$$\begin{array}{r} 2 \\ + \ 4 \\ \hline \end{array}$$

A piece of chalk is 5 blocks **long**
and a banana 10 blocks **long**.
Total length: _____ blocks

$$\begin{array}{r} 5 \\ + \ 10 \\ \hline \end{array}$$

Using a Grid to Measure (i)

Fill in the blank with the correct letter.

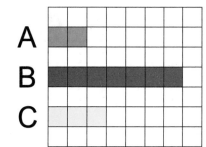

Bar _____ is
3 units **long**.

(☐ = 1 unit)

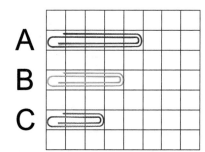

Paper clip _____ is
5 units **long**.

(☐ = 1 unit)

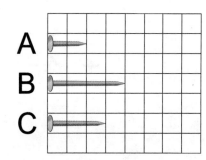

Nail _____ is
4 units **long**.

(☐ = 1 unit)

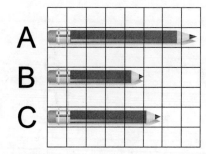

Pencil _____ is
8 units **long**.

(☐ = 1 unit)

Length and Distance I

Fill in the blank with the correct name.

Dan   Daisy   Leah

(☐ = 1 unit)

_____ is 7 units **tall**.

_____ is 6 units **tall**.

_____ is the **tallest** person.

_____ is **shorter** than Dan.

★ Star Question

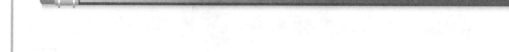

Take a guess!

1 paper clip is _____ nails **long**.

1 eraser is _____ paper clips **long**.

1 pencil is _____ erasers **long**.

1 pencil is _____ nails **long**.

Length and Distance I

Measures Tools – Non-Standard Measuring Tools

Directions: Cut out the groups of objects around the dotted black line. Use the non-standard units to measure items around your home. Try the ideas on the next page, or think of your own!

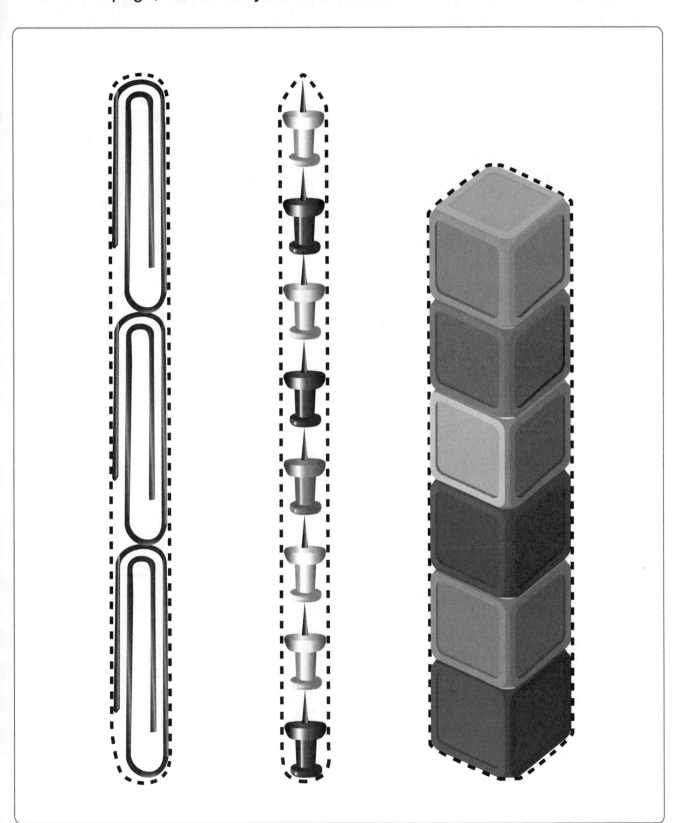

Ideas to try!

1. How many blocks tall is your bed? How many blocks wide is your doorway?
2. How many paper clips long is the distance from your elbow to your shoulder?
3. How many thumbtacks long is a cell phone? How about a dollar bill?
4. Use an inch or centimeter ruler to measure the height of the stack of blocks. What is the actual measurement?

Congratulations! Great Work!

Your Name

You have successfully completed the requirements for the workbook practice section of:

GRADE 1 LEVEL 1 MEASURES

Professor Mugo

PLANETii Director of Learning

Est since 2000

Planet-ii

login @

Don't forget to claim your stars and iipoints online.

Shapes and Space

LEVEL 1

This SHAPES AND SPACE section introduces students to different kinds of lines, including straight lines and curved lines that can be used to make different shapes.

STRAIGHT LINES AND CURVED LINES

- Drawing Straight Lines and Curved Lines
- Finding Straight Lines and Curved Lines in Shapes
- Activities with Straight Lines and Curved Lines
- Drawing Shapes

Straight Lines and Curved Lines

Straight Lines and Curved Lines
LEVEL 1 SHAPES AND SPACE

Learn It!

Straight Lines ——— / |

Curved Lines ⌣ ∿ (

Straight lines are used to make polygons.

A triangle is made up of 3 straight lines.

A square is made up of 4 straight lines.

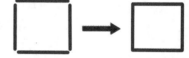

A circle is made up of curved lines.

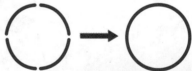

Use It!

Which figure is made of exactly 4
straight lines and 2 **curved lines**?

A   B   C   D   E

....

4 **straight lines** and 2 **curved lines**.
Figure A is the only one made up of exactly

Answer

....

Which figure is made of exactly 5
straight lines and no **curved lines**?

A   B   C   D   E

....

It's a pentagon.
Figure B has 5 **straight lines** and no **curved lines**.

Answer

Straight Lines and Curved Lines

Practice drawing curved lines and straight lines.

Straight Lines and Curved Lines

Draw a line around the object to complete each picture.
Next to it, circle the word **straight** or **curved** to show
what kind of line you drew.

straight

curved

straight

curved

straight

curved

straight

curved

Draw a line around the object to complete each picture. Next to it, circle the word **straight** or **curved** to show what kind of line you drew.

straight

curved

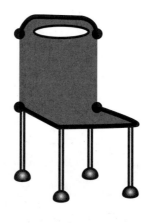

straight

curved

straight

curved

straight

curved

Finding Straight Lines and Curved Lines in Shapes (i)

Circle all the figures with at least one **curved** line.

Circle all the figures with at least one **straight** line.

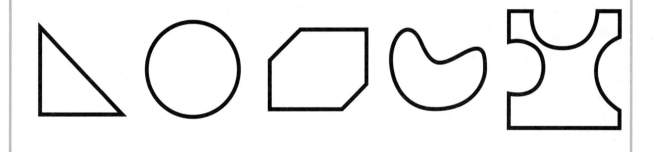

Circle the figure with exactly 2 **curved** lines.

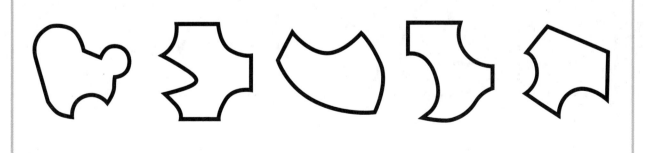

Draw a ◯ under the figure(s) with only **curved** lines.

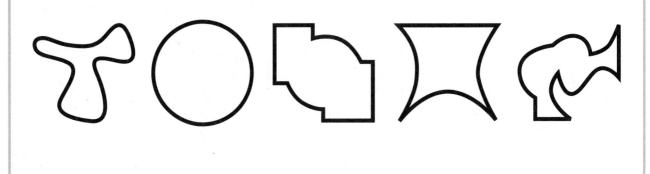

Draw a ☐ under the figure(s) with only **straight** lines.

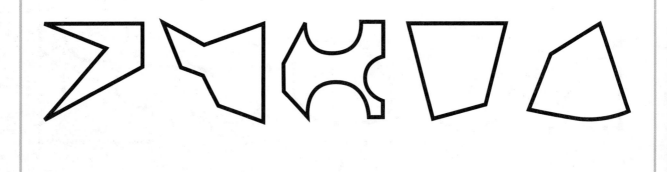

Draw a ⌓ under the figure(s) with both **curved** lines and **straight** lines.

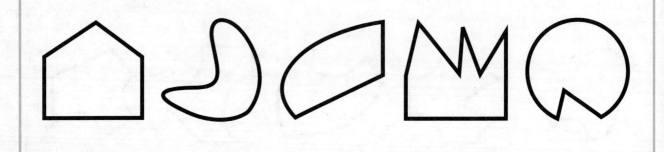

Color the figures with curved lines red.
Color the figures with straight lines blue.

Finding Straight Lines and Curved Lines in Shapes (iv)

How many **straight lines** are there on each shape?

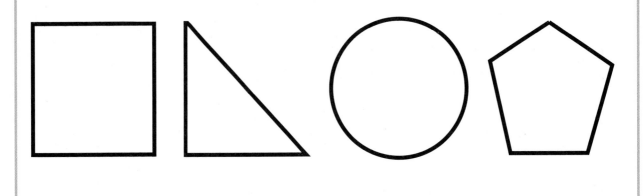

_____   _____   _____   _____

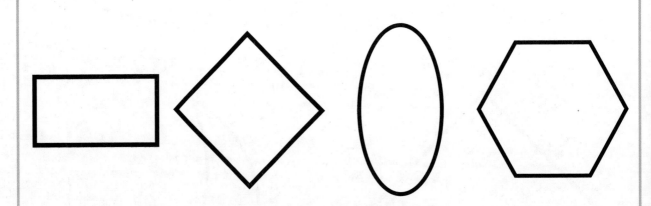

_____   _____   _____   _____

Straight Lines and Curved Lines

Trace to complete each shape. Did you draw **curved lines** or **straight lines**? Write your answers.

Trace 3 more **curved lines** to add more **curves** to the rainbow. Then, color the rainbow.

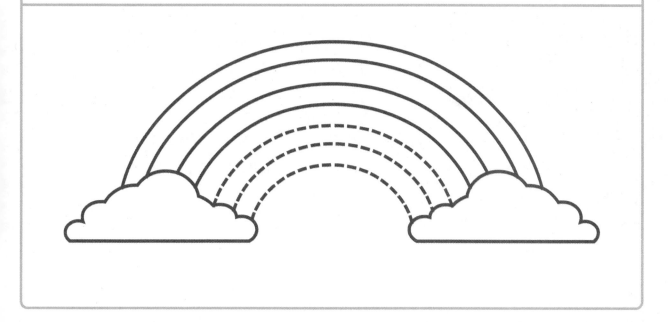

Draw the following objects in the box. On the line, write whether the object has **straight lines** or **curved lines** or both.

tennis ball

_____

eye ball

_____

star

_____

candy cane

_____

Flower

_____

Table

_____

Draw your own closed shapes using:

2 straight lines &
1 curved line

3 curved lines

3 straight lines &
1 curved line

4 curved lines

4 straight lines

2 straight lines &
2 curved lines

Star Question

Draw a **straight line**, a **curved line**, or a shape to complete each pattern.

Line and Dot Grid Game

Find a friend and two different colored pens, markers, or pencils. Take turns connecting two dots until you form a complete square. Whoever draws the last line to close the square, should write his or her first initial inside the square. Continue play until you cannot make any more squares. Count the initials to see who has the most squares. Make your own board and play again!

Straight Lines and Curved Lines

Congratulations!
Great Work!

Planet ii. Est. since 2000

Your Name

You have successfully completed the requirements
for the workbook practice section of:

**GRADE 1 LEVEL 1
SHAPES AND SPACE**

Professor Mugo

PLANETii Director of Learning

Please enter this
code to gain six stars
from your SmartMath Practice
round. These stars will increase
your iiPoints and assist you when
you are ready to challenge for
this topic at

www.britannicasmartmath.com
/workbook

8210

5

login@

www.britannicasmartmath.com/workbook

username

password

Don't forget to claim your stars and iipoints online.

You are top of the line!

Awesome Work
with Shapes and Space!

Count, Read, and Write Numbers 1-10

Match the number to the set with the same number of objects.

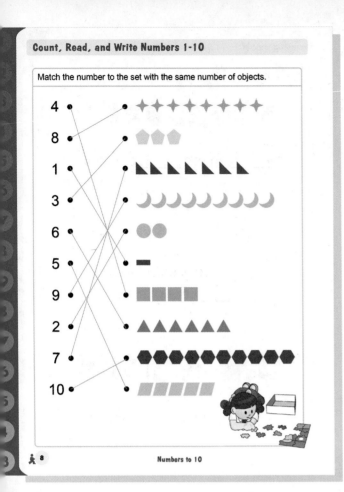

Writing Numbers 1 to 10

10

Trace and write the numbers 1 - 10 in number and word form.

1	1	one	one	one
2	2	two	two	two
3	3	three	three	three
4	4	four	four	four
5	5	five	five	five
6	6	six	six	six
7	7	seven	seven	seven
8	8	eight	eight	eight
9	9	nine	nine	nine
10	10	ten	ten	ten

Counting and Writing Numbers (i)

Count and write how many in number and word form.

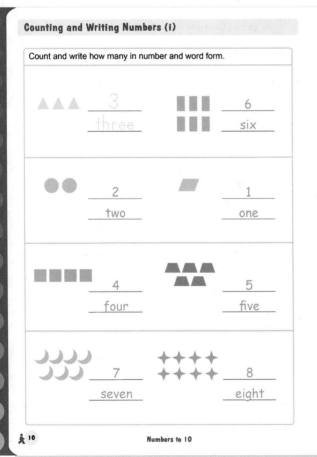

Counting and Writing Numbers (ii)

10

Count and write how many in number form and word form.

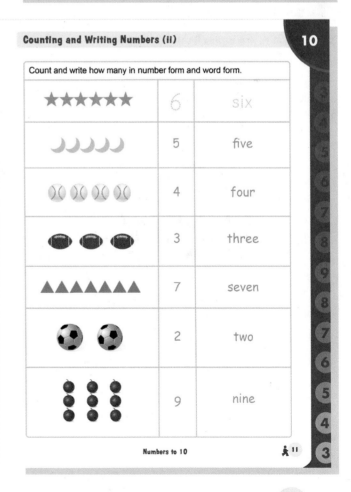

Answer Key

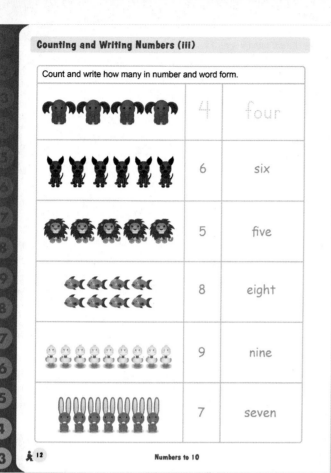

Count and write how many in number and word form.

	4	four
	6	six
	5	five
	8	eight
	9	nine
	7	seven

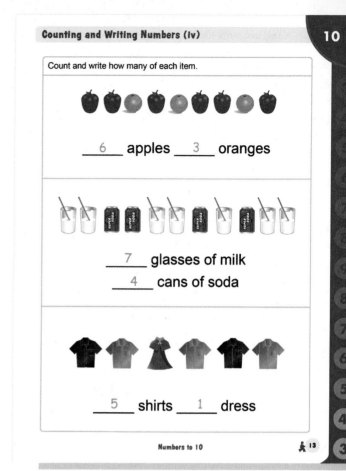

Count and write how many of each item.

____6__ apples ___3__ oranges

____7__ glasses of milk
____4__ cans of soda

____5__ shirts ___1___ dress

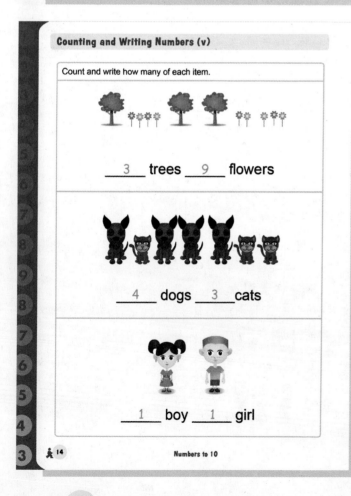

Count and write how many of each item.

___3___ trees __9___ flowers

___4___ dogs __3___ cats

___1__ boy ___1__ girl

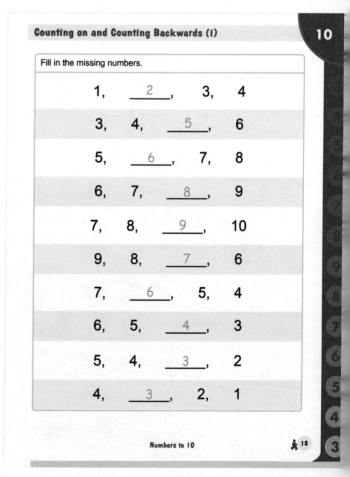

Fill in the missing numbers.

1, ___2___, 3, 4

3, 4, ___5___, 6

5, ___6___, 7, 8

6, 7, ___8___, 9

7, 8, ___9___, 10

9, 8, ___7___, 6

7, ___6___, 5, 4

6, 5, ___4___, 3

5, 4, ___3___, 2

4, ___3___, 2, 1

Answer Key

Counting on and Counting Backwards (ii)

Fill in the missing numbers.

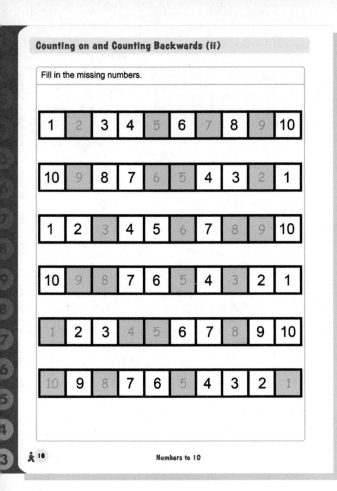

Counting on (i)

Look at the counting sequence in each row. In the last box, draw the correct number of objects to complete each sequence.

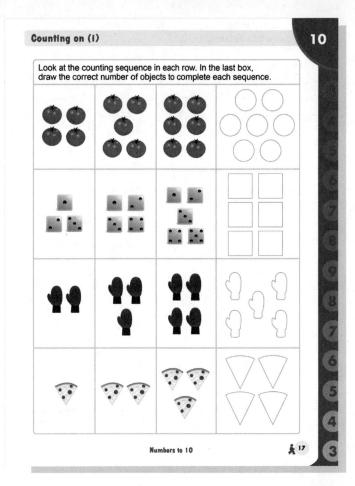

Counting on (ii)

Look at the counting sequence in each row. In the empty box, draw the correct number of objects to complete each sequence.

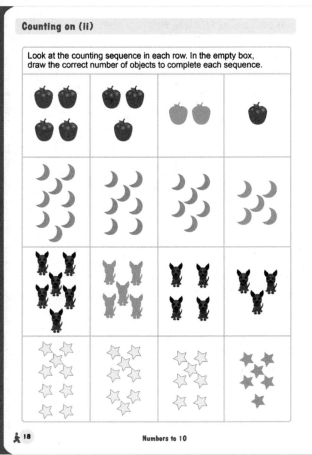

Even and Odd Numbers (i)

Circle the even number in each row.
Even numbers can be found by skip-counting from number 2.

1,   (2,)   3,   5,   7

3,   (4,)   5,   7,   9

3,   5,   (6,)   7,   9

3,   5,   7,   (8,)   9

3,   5,   7,   9,   (10)

1,   3,   5,   7,   (8)

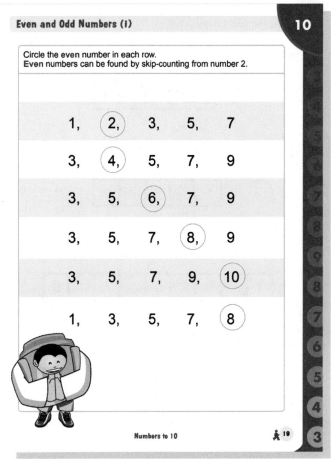

Answer Key

Even and Odd Numbers (ii)

Circle the odd number in each row.
Odd numbers can be found by skip-counting from number 1.

2, ③, 6, 8, 10

①, 2, 4, 6, 8

2, 4, 6, ⑦, 10

2, 4, ⑤, 6, 8

2, ③, 4, 6, 8

4, 6, 8, ⑨, 10

4, 6, ⑦, 8, 10

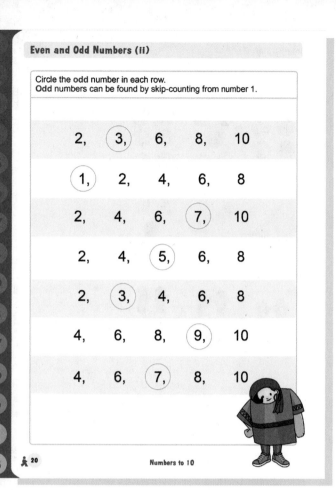

Numbers to 10

Even and Odd Numbers (iii)

Circle the even numbers. Draw a box around the odd numbers.

How many **odd** numbers in all? __10__

How many **even** numbers in all? __10__

Numbers to 10

Even and Odd Numbers (iv)

Fill in the other even numbers.

| 2 | 4 | 6 | 8 | 10 |

Fill in the other odd numbers.

| 1 | 3 | 5 | 7 | 9 |

Fill in the missing even numbers.

| 1 | 2 | 3 | 4 | 5 | 6 | 7 | 8 | 9 |

Fill in the missing odd numbers.

| 2 | 3 | 4 | 5 | 6 | 7 | 8 | 9 | 10 |

Numbers to 10

Comparing Groups of Objects (i)

Count. Circle the group with fewer objects.

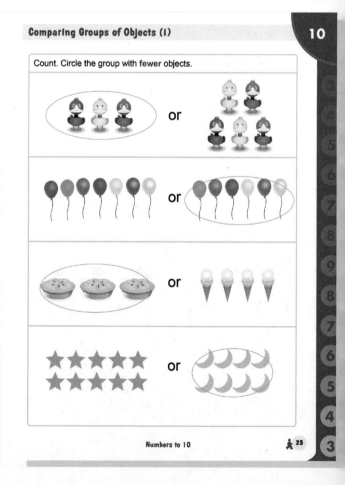

Numbers to 10

Answer Key

Comparing Groups of Objects (ii)

Count. Circle the group with more objects.

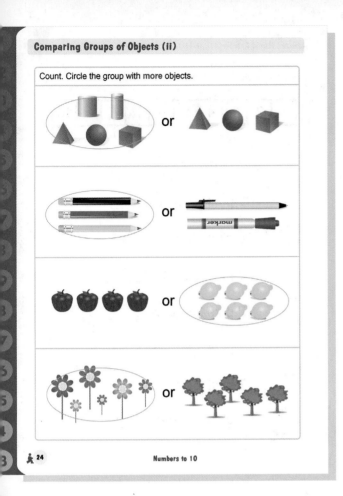

Adding Groups of Objects Together (i)

Count and write how many in each box.

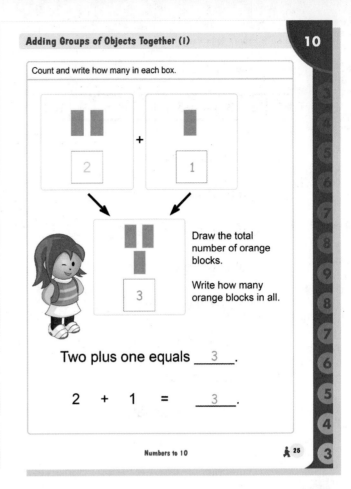

Draw the total number of orange blocks.

Write how many orange blocks in all.

Two plus one equals ___3___.

2 + 1 = ___3___.

Adding Groups of Objects Together (ii)

Count and write how many in each box.

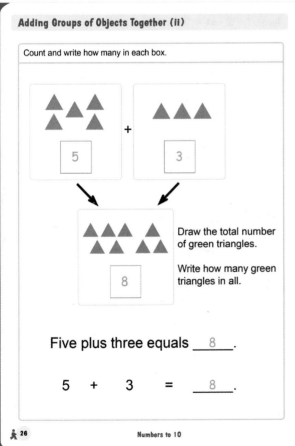

Draw the total number of green triangles.

Write how many green triangles in all.

Five plus three equals ___8___.

5 + 3 = ___8___.

Comparing Groups of Objects (iii)

How many objects are missing? Draw the objects that are missing to make the groups equal. Write the number to show how many objects you added to make the groups equal.

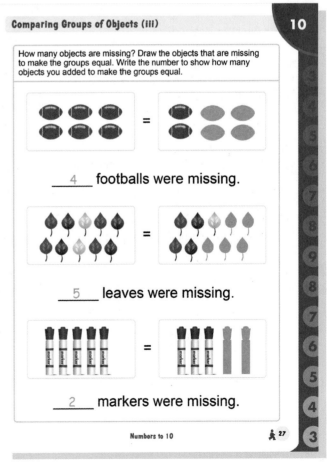

___4___ footballs were missing.

___5___ leaves were missing.

___2___ markers were missing.

Answer Key

Adding Numbers Together (i)

Write the correct number on the line to finish each sentence.

1	2	3	4	5	6	7	8	9	10

9 plus 1 more equals __10__.

3 plus 2 more equals __5__.

5 plus 4 more equals __9__.

3 plus 6 more equals __9__.

2 plus 7 more equals __9__.

5 plus 4 more equals __9__.

6 plus 3 more equals __9__.

8 plus 2 more equals __10__.

28   Numbers to 10

Adding Numbers Together (ii)

Write the correct number on the line to finish each sentence.

1	2	3	4	5	6	7	8	9	10

3 plus 1 equals __4__.

5 plus 4 equals __9__.

9 plus 1 equals __10__.

6 plus 2 equals __8__.

2 plus 3 equals __5__.

1 plus 4 equals __5__.

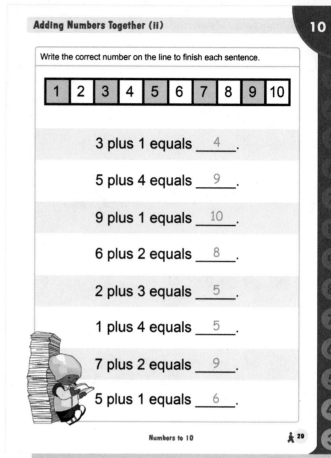

7 plus 2 equals __9__.

5 plus 1 equals __6__.

Numbers to 10   29

★ Star Question (cont'd)

There are __7__ lemons.

There are __6__ fish.

There are __5__ flowers.

Is there an **even** or an **odd** number of frogs?
__odd__

Is there an **even** or an **odd** number of bananas? __even__

The number of frogs and the number of fish make __9__ animals in all.

__3__ frogs + __6__ fish = __9__ animals

Numbers to 10   31

Count, Read, and Write Numbers 11-20

Trace and write the numbers and words from 11-20.

11	11	eleven	eleven	eleven
12	12	twelve	twelve	twelve
13	13	thirteen	thirteen	thirteen
14	14	fourteen	fourteen	fourteen
15	15	fifteen	fifteen	fifteen
16	16	sixteen	sixteen	sixteen
17	17	seventeen	seventeen	seventeen
18	18	eighteen	eighteen	eighteen
19	19	nineteen	nineteen	nineteen
20	20	twenty	twenty	twenty

34   Numbers to 20

Answer Key

Number Words (I)

Match the number to the word.

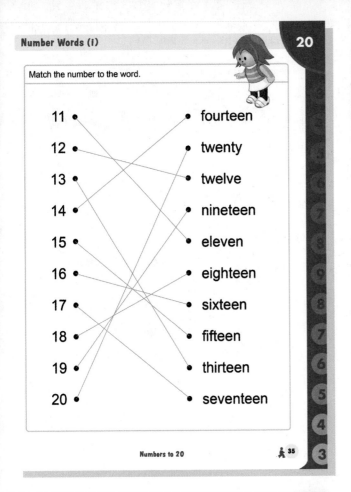

Numbers to 20   🚶 35

Number Words (ii)

Write the numbers in words.

1	one	2	two
3	three	4	four
5	five	6	six
7	seven	8	eight
9	nine	10	ten
16	sixteen	17	seventeen
18	eighteen	19	nineteen
20	twenty	15	fifteen
12	twelve	11	eleven
14	fourteen	13	thirteen

🚶 36   Numbers to 20

Number Words (iii)

Count the objects. Write how many in number and word form.

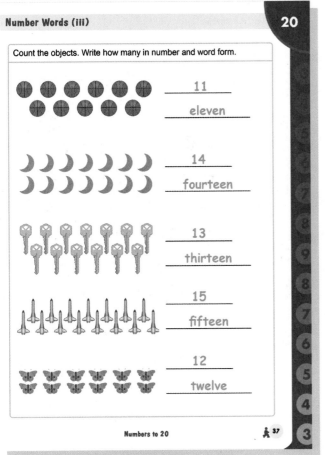

11
eleven

14
fourteen

13
thirteen

15
fifteen

12
twelve

Numbers to 20   🚶 37

Number Words (iv)

Count the objects. Write how many in number and word form.

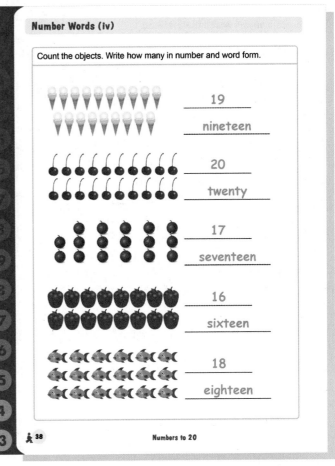

19
nineteen

20
twenty

17
seventeen

16
sixteen

18
eighteen

🚶 38   Numbers to 20

Answer Key   🚶143

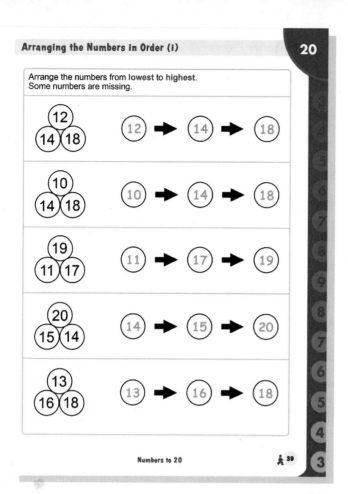

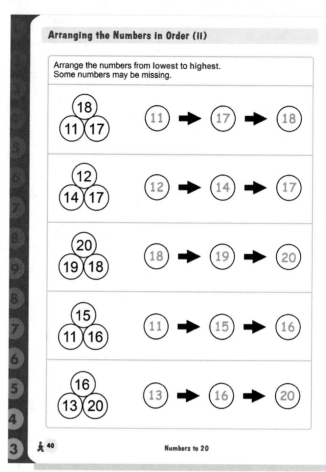

Counting on and Counting Backwards

20

Fill in the missing numbers.

11, _12_, 13, 14, 15, 16

15, 16, _17_, 18, 19, 20

12, 13, 14, _15_, 16, 17

10, 11, 12, 13, _14_, 15

20, 19, _18_, 17, 16, 15

18, 17, 16, 15, 14, _13_

15, _14_, 13, 12, 11, 10

17, 16, 15, _14_, 13, 12

_16_, 15, 14, 13, 12, 11

Ordinal Numbers (i)

Practice writing ordinal numbers.

1st	1st	first	first	first
2nd	2nd	second	second	second
3rd	3rd	third	third	third
4th	4th	fourth	fourth	fourth
5th	5th	fifth	fifth	fifth
6th	6th	sixth	sixth	sixth
7th	7th	seventh	seventh	seventh
8th	8th	eighth	eighth	eighth
9th	9th	ninth	ninth	ninth
10th	10th	tenth	tenth	tenth

Answer Key

Match the number to the word.

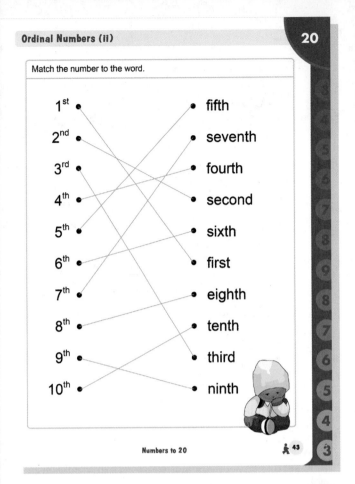

1st • fifth
2nd • seventh
3rd • fourth
4th • second
5th • sixth
6th • first
7th • eighth
8th • tenth
9th • third
10th • ninth

Numbers to 20   43

Circle the object that is in the 2nd place.

1st 2nd 3rd 4th 5th

Circle the object that is in the 3rd place.

Circle the object that is in the 4th place.

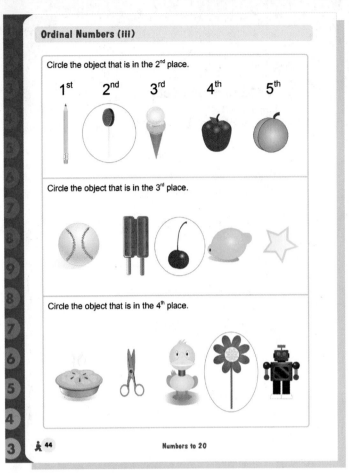

44   Numbers to 20

Count and write how many in each box.
Draw the total number of objects in the last box.

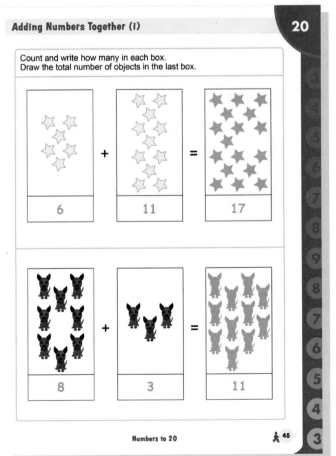

6   +   11   =   17

8   +   3   =   11

Numbers to 20   45

Count and write how many in each box.
Draw the total number of objects in the last box.

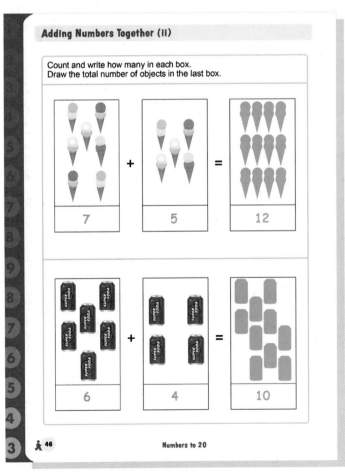

7   +   5   =   12

6   +   4   =   10

46   Numbers to 20

Answer Key   145

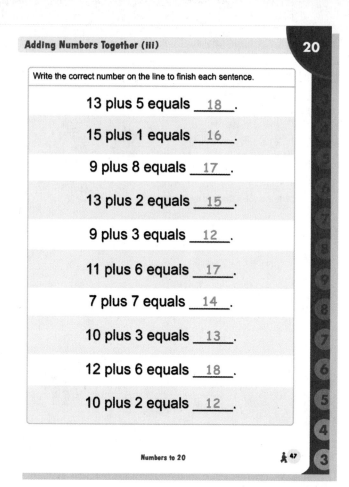

Adding Numbers Together (iii)

Write the correct number on the line to finish each sentence.

13 plus 5 equals __18__.

15 plus 1 equals __16__.

9 plus 8 equals __17__.

13 plus 2 equals __15__.

9 plus 3 equals __12__.

11 plus 6 equals __17__.

7 plus 7 equals __14__.

10 plus 3 equals __13__.

12 plus 6 equals __18__.

10 plus 2 equals __12__.

Numbers to 20　47

Review (i)

Count the objects and write how many.

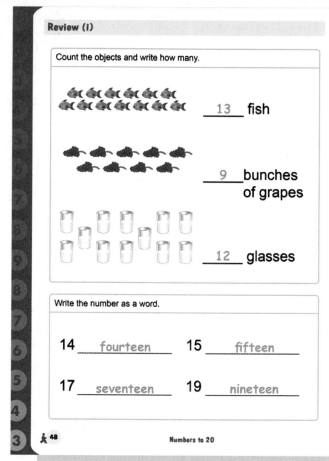

__13__ fish

__9__ bunches of grapes

__12__ glasses

Write the number as a word.

14 ___fourteen___　15 ___fifteen___

17 ___seventeen___　19 ___nineteen___

48　Numbers to 20

Review (ii)

Add and write the correct number on the line to finish each sentence.

13 plus 5 equals __18__.

15 plus 1 equals __16__.

9 plus 8 equals __17__.

Match the number to the word.

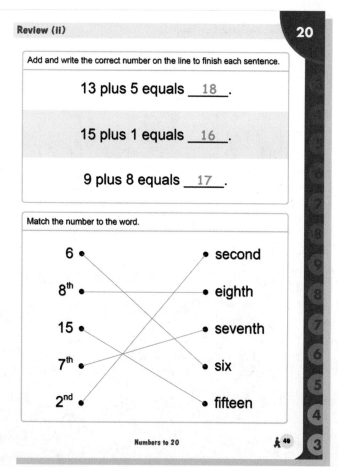

6 •   • second

8th •   • eighth

15 •   • seventh

7th •   • six

2nd •   • fifteen

Numbers to 20　49

★ Star Question

Solve.

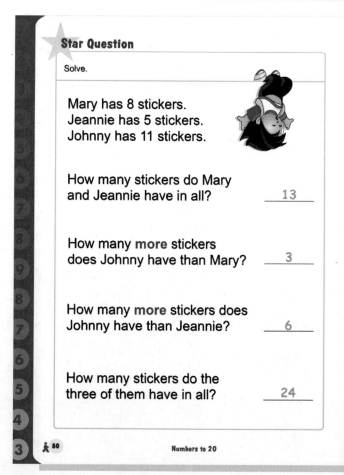

Mary has 8 stickers.
Jeannie has 5 stickers.
Johnny has 11 stickers.

How many stickers do Mary and Jeannie have in all?　__13__

How many **more** stickers does Johnny have than Mary?　__3__

How many **more** stickers does Johnny have than Jeannie?　__6__

How many stickers do the three of them have in all?　__24__

50　Numbers to 20

Answer Key

Putting Together and Taking Away Objects (i)

Amanda has 5 flowers.
Caroline has 2 flowers.

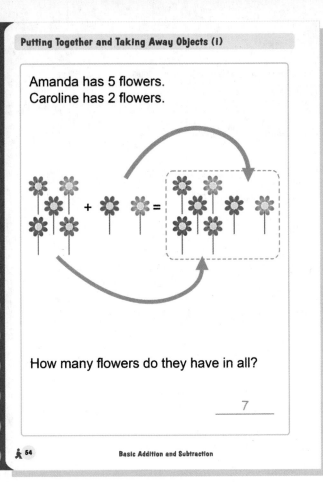

How many flowers do they have in all?

_____7_____

Basic Addition and Subtraction

Putting Together and Taking Away Objects (ii)   +/−

Sam has 6 toy cars.
Jim has 8 toy cars.

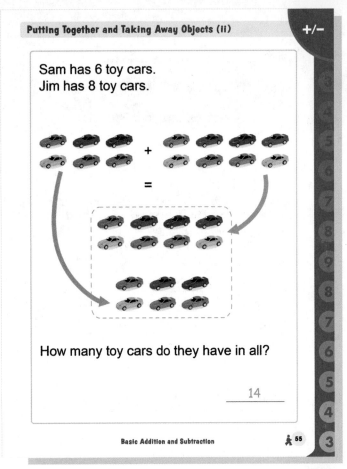

How many toy cars do they have in all?

_____14_____

Basic Addition and Subtraction

Putting Together and Taking Away Objects (iii)

There were 5 shirts in Joe's closet.
He gave away 2 shirts.

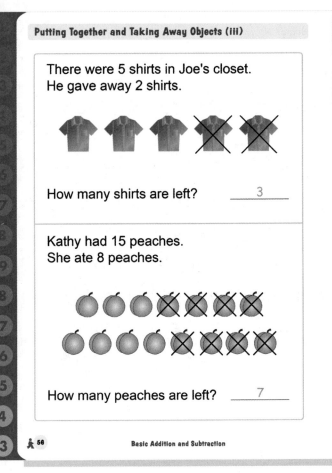

How many shirts are left? _____3_____

Kathy had 15 peaches.
She ate 8 peaches.

How many peaches are left? _____7_____

Basic Addition and Subtraction

Putting Together and Taking Away Objects (iv)   +/−

Write the numbers to help solve the picture equations.

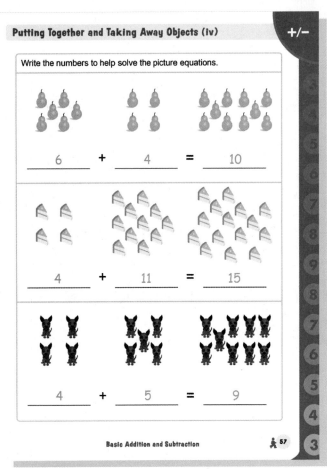

_____6_____ + _____4_____ = _____10_____

_____4_____ + _____11_____ = _____15_____

_____4_____ + _____5_____ = _____9_____

Basic Addition and Subtraction

Answer Key

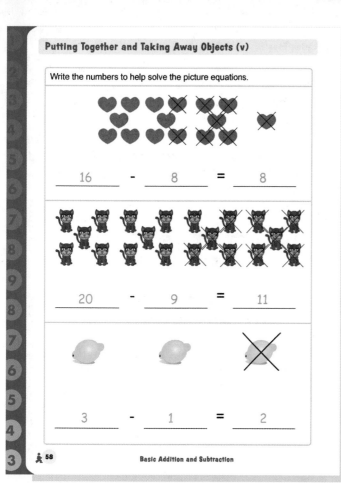

Putting Together and Taking Away Objects (v)

Write the numbers to help solve the picture equations.

16 - 8 = 8

20 - 9 = 11

3 - 1 = 2

Basic Addition and Subtraction

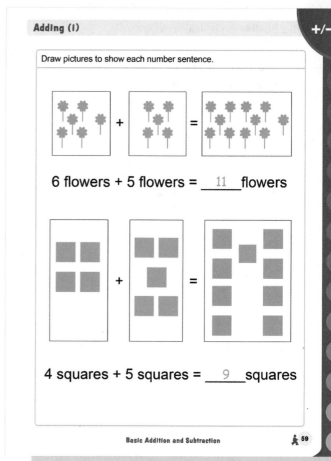

Adding (i)

+/−

Draw pictures to show each number sentence.

6 flowers + 5 flowers = 11 flowers

4 squares + 5 squares = 9 squares

Basic Addition and Subtraction

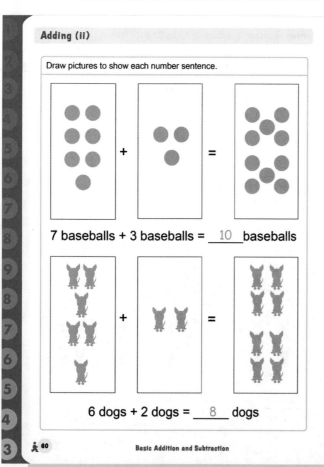

Adding (ii)

Draw pictures to show each number sentence.

7 baseballs + 3 baseballs = 10 baseballs

6 dogs + 2 dogs = 8 dogs

Basic Addition and Subtraction

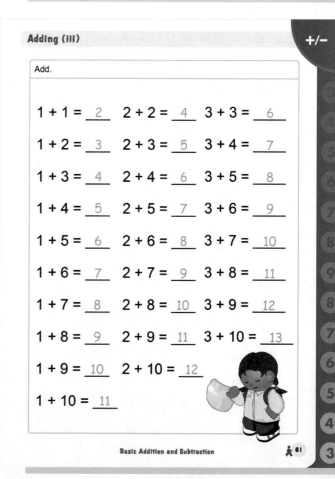

Adding (iii)

+/−

Add.

1 + 1 = 2	2 + 2 = 4	3 + 3 = 6
1 + 2 = 3	2 + 3 = 5	3 + 4 = 7
1 + 3 = 4	2 + 4 = 6	3 + 5 = 8
1 + 4 = 5	2 + 5 = 7	3 + 6 = 9
1 + 5 = 6	2 + 6 = 8	3 + 7 = 10
1 + 6 = 7	2 + 7 = 9	3 + 8 = 11
1 + 7 = 8	2 + 8 = 10	3 + 9 = 12
1 + 8 = 9	2 + 9 = 11	3 + 10 = 13
1 + 9 = 10	2 + 10 = 12	
1 + 10 = 11		

Basic Addition and Subtraction

Answer Key

Adding (iv)

Add.

$5 + 5 = \underline{10}$ $6 + 6 = \underline{12}$ $7 + 7 = \underline{14}$

$5 + 6 = \underline{11}$ $6 + 7 = \underline{13}$ $7 + 8 = \underline{15}$

$5 + 7 = \underline{12}$ $6 + 8 = \underline{14}$ $7 + 9 = \underline{16}$

$5 + 8 = \underline{13}$ $6 + 9 = \underline{15}$ $7 + 10 = \underline{17}$

$5 + 9 = \underline{14}$ $6 + 10 = \underline{16}$

$5 + 10 = \underline{15}$

$8 + 8 = \underline{16}$ $9 + 9 = \underline{18}$

$8 + 9 = \underline{17}$ $9 + 10 = \underline{19}$

$8 + 10 = \underline{18}$

Basic Addition and Subtraction

Subtracting (i)

+/−

Write the correct number on the line to show the **difference** between the groups of objects.

There are 12 apples and 7 lemons.

$12 - 7 = \underline{5}$

There are __5__ more apples than there are lemons.

Subtracting (ii)

Write the correct number on the line to show the **difference** between the groups of objects.

There are 9 spoons and 6 forks.

$9 - 6 = \underline{3}$

There are __3__ more spoons than there are forks.

Basic Addition and Subtraction

Subtracting (iii)

+/−

Subtract.

$12 - 2 = \underline{10}$ $12 - 1 = \underline{11}$

$12 - 4 = \underline{8}$ $12 - 3 = \underline{9}$

$12 - 6 = \underline{6}$ $12 - 5 = \underline{7}$

$12 - 8 = \underline{4}$ $12 - 7 = \underline{5}$

$12 - 10 = \underline{2}$ $12 - 9 = \underline{3}$

$16 - 3 = \underline{13}$ $12 - 11 = \underline{1}$

$16 - 6 = \underline{10}$ $16 - 4 = \underline{12}$

$16 - 9 = \underline{7}$ $16 - 8 = \underline{8}$

$16 - 2 = \underline{14}$ $16 - 12 = \underline{4}$

Answer Key

Subtracting (iv)

Subtract.

18 - 1 = __17__   18 - 11 = __7__

18 - 2 = __16__   18 - 12 = __6__

18 - 3 = __15__   18 - 13 = __5__

18 - 4 = __14__   18 - 14 = __4__

18 - 5 = __13__   18 - 15 = __3__

18 - 6 = __12__   18 - 16 = __2__

18 - 7 = __11__   18 - 17 = __1__

18 - 8 = __10__

18 - 9 = __9__

18 - 10 = __8__

Adding up to 18

Add.

5 + 3 = __8__   12 + 3 = __15__

2 + 6 = __8__   9 + 5 = __14__

3 + 8 = __11__   6 + 7 = __13__

7 + 9 = __16__   6 + 8 = __14__

4 + 8 = __12__   5 + 7 = __12__

5 + 6 = __11__   4 + 6 = __10__

12 + 4 = __16__   3 + 9 = __12__

10 + 5 = __15__   11 + 5 = __16__

13 + 4 = __17__   13 + 4 = __17__

11 + 6 = __17__   10 + 8 = __18__

15 + 1 = __16__   9 + 7 = __16__

Subtracting up to 18

Subtract.

15 - 4 = __11__   14 - 7 = __7__

12 - 8 = __4__   15 - 9 = __6__

14 - 3 = __11__   18 - 3 = __15__

10 - 6 = __4__   16 - 2 = __14__

13 - 7 = __6__   17 - 2 = __15__

12 - 5 = __7__   11 - 3 = __8__

8 - 4 = __4__   10 - 7 = __3__

14 - 8 = __6__   13 - 6 = __7__

9 - 4 = __5__   17 - 4 = __13__

6 - 2 = __4__   11 - 8 = __3__

12 - 3 = __9__   13 - 5 = __8__

Adding and Subtracting up to 18

Pick a number from the bubble to complete each number sentence.

15   10   3   9   5   2   11   12   8   16

11 - 3 = __8__   15 - 3 = __12__

10 + __2__ = 12   __5__ + 4 = 9

8 + 7 = __15__   8 + 2 = __10__

14 - 3 = __11__   18 - 15 = __3__

7 + __9__ = 16   4 + 12 = __16__

Answer Key

The Number Zero (i)

How many are left?

before:

There are ___0___ glasses of milk left.

before:

There are ___0___ cookies left.

before:

There are ___0___ cakes left.

before:

There are ___0___ grapes left.

The Number Zero (ii)   +/−

A number plus or minus 0 equals the number.
Add. Adding 0 is like adding nothing.

$18 + 0 =$ ___18___ $0 + 6 =$ ___6___

$4 + 0 =$ ___4___ $0 + 3 =$ ___3___

$9 + 0 =$ ___9___ $0 + 15 =$ ___15___

$13 + 0 =$ ___13___ $0 + 10 =$ ___10___

A number minus that same number equals 0.
Subtract. Subtracting 0 is like subtracting nothing.

$14 - 0 =$ ___14___ $14 - 14 =$ ___0___

$5 - 5 =$ ___0___ $5 - 0 =$ ___5___

$7 - 7 =$ ___0___ $7 - 0 =$ ___7___

$16 - 16 =$ ___0___ $16 - 0 =$ ___16___

Addition and Subtraction: Working Together (i)

Write how many below the pictures.

___3___ cupcakes + ___4___ cupcakes = ___7___ cupcakes

___7___ cupcakes in all − ___3___ cupcakes = ___4___ cupcakes

___8___ pencils + ___4___ pencils = ___12___ pencils

___12___ pencils in all − ___8___ pencils = ___4___ pencils

Addition and Subtraction: Working Together (ii)   +/−

Write how many below the pictures.

___6___ apples + ___3___ apples = ___9___ apples

___9___ apples in all − ___3___ apples = ___6___ apples

___4___ apples + ___8___ apples = ___12___ apples

___12___ apples in all − ___4___ apples = ___8___ apples

Answer Key   151

Addition and Subtraction: Working Together (iii)

Pick a number from the bubble to complete each number sentence.

10   12
4   3   15
9   13   7
3

10 + __4__ = 14 and 14 - 4 = __10__

6 + 3 = __9__ and 9 - __3__ = 6

5 + __7__ = 12 and __12__ - 7 = 5

__13__ + 2 = 15 and __15__ - 2 = 13

Changing the Order in Addition (Commutative Property) (i) +/−

Write the missing numbers below the pictures.

__2__ + __3__ = __3__ + __2__

__4__ + __3__ = __3__ + __4__

__5__ + __6__ = __6__ + __5__

Changing the Order in Addition (Commutative Property) (ii)

Write the missing numbers and draw the missing pictures.

__7__   __2__   __2__   __7__

__12__   __5__   __5__   __12__

__10__   __8__   __8__   __10__

Review   +/−

Add to find how many hearts in all.

__14__ hearts + __3__ hearts = __17__ hearts in all.

Count and write the number to show how many pairs of pants in all.
Cross out 3 pairs of pants. Count how many are left and write the answer.

__12__ pairs of pants in all - 3 pairs of pants = __9__ pairs of pants

Add.

13 + 5 = __18__   9 + 7 = __16__

6 + 4 = __10__   8 + 6 = __14__

7 + 6 = __13__   14 + 3 = __17__

Answer Key

Star Question

Solve.

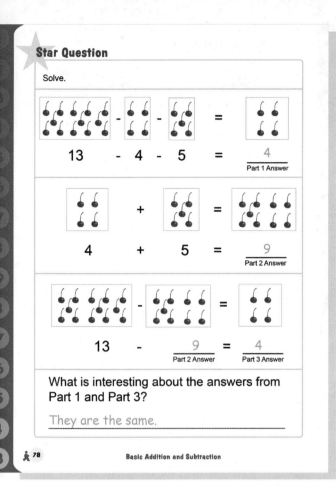

$$13 - 4 - 5 = \underline{4}$$
Part 1 Answer

$$4 + 5 = \underline{9}$$
Part 2 Answer

$$13 - \underline{9} = \underline{4}$$
Part 2 Answer   Part 3 Answer

What is interesting about the answers from Part 1 and Part 3?

They are the same.

👤 78   Basic Addition and Subtraction

Draw a ✔ next to the longer object.

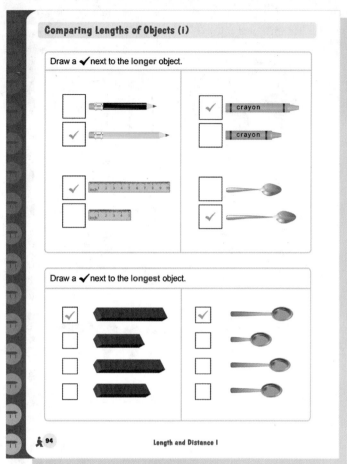

Draw a ✔ next to the longest object.

👤 94   Length and Distance I

Comparing Lengths of Objects (ii)

Draw a ✔ next to the shorter object.

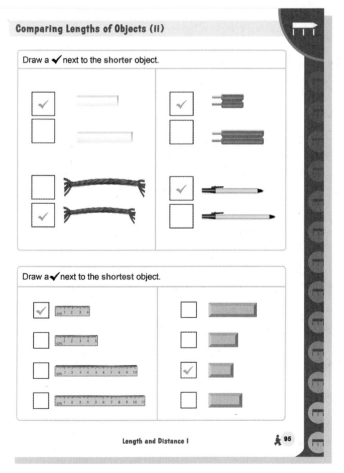

Draw a ✔ next to the shortest object.

Length and Distance I   👤 95

Comparing Lengths of Objects (iii)

Circle the longer object in each pair.

An (airplane) or a bus?

A (jump rope) or a ruler?

An eraser or a (comb)?

A stamp or an (envelope)?

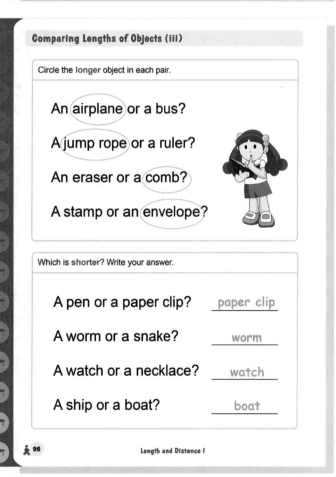

Which is shorter? Write your answer.

A pen or a paper clip?   paper clip

A worm or a snake?   worm

A watch or a necklace?   watch

A ship or a boat?   boat

👤 96   Length and Distance I

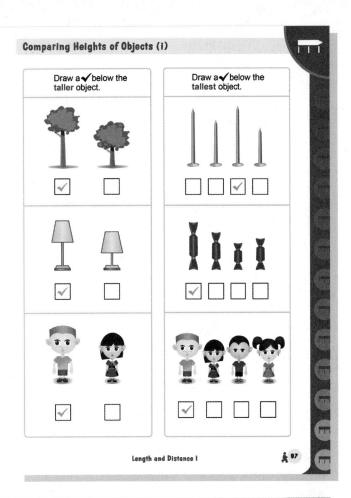

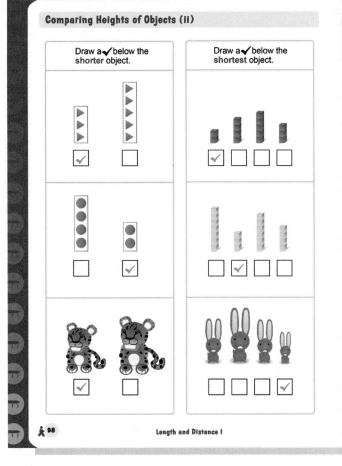

Which is taller? Write your answer.

A mountain or a bookshelf? ____mountain____

A milk carton or a chair? ____chair____

A computer or a refrigerator? ____refrigerator____

A baby or an adult? ____adult____

Which is shorter? Write your answer.

A lamp or a house? ____lamp____

A flagpole or a candle? ____candle____

A soda can or a trash can? ____soda can____

A giraffe or a dog? ____dog____

Use the diagram to answer the following questions.

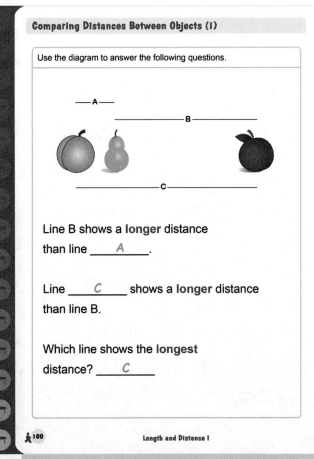

Line B shows a **longer** distance than line ____A____.

Line ____C____ shows a **longer** distance than line B.

Which line shows the **longest** distance? ____C____

Comparing Distances Between Objects (ii)

Use the diagram to answer the following questions.

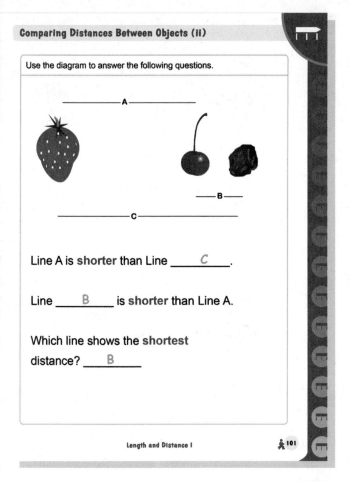

Line A is **shorter than** Line ___C___.

Line ___B___ is **shorter than** Line A.

Which line shows the **shortest** distance? ___B___

Comparing Distances Between Objects (iii)

Draw a ✔ next to the **longest** distance.

☐ Your head to your shoulders	✔ Your bedroom to your school
OR	OR
✔ Your head to your toes	☐ Your bedroom to your bathroom

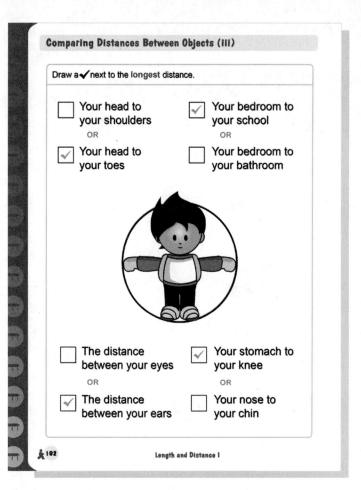

☐ The distance between your eyes	✔ Your stomach to your knee
OR	OR
✔ The distance between your ears	☐ Your nose to your chin

Using Everyday Objects to Measure (i)

How many paper clips **long** are the objects?

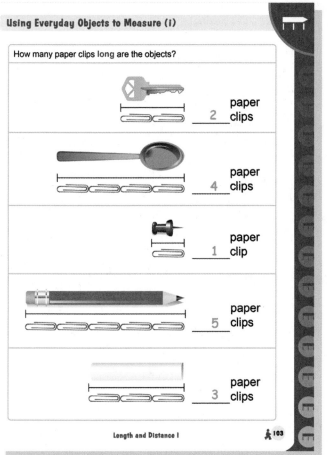

___2___ paper clips

___4___ paper clips

___1___ paper clip

___5___ paper clips

___3___ paper clips

Using Everyday Objects to Measure (ii)

How many thumb tacks **tall** is each object?

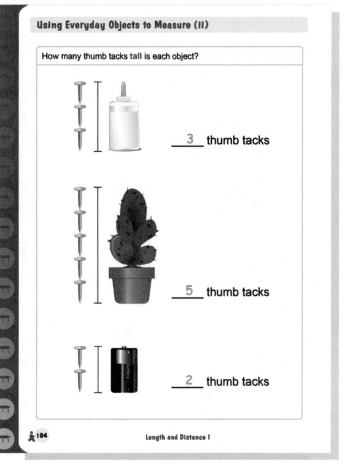

___3___ thumb tacks

___5___ thumb tacks

___2___ thumb tacks

Answer Key

What is the distance between each pair of objects?
How many paper clips or blocks long is the distance?

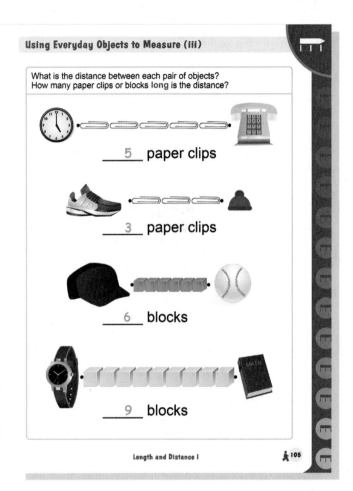

_____5_____ paper clips

_____3_____ paper clips

_____6_____ blocks

_____9_____ blocks

Complete each measurement with the correct number.

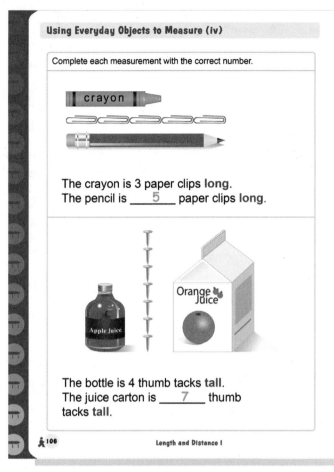

The crayon is 3 paper clips **long**.
The pencil is _____5_____ paper clips **long**.

The bottle is 4 thumb tacks **tall**.
The juice carton is _____7_____ thumb tacks **tall**.

What is the total length of the two items added together?

A pencil is 7 blocks **long** and a crayon is 4 blocks **long**.
Total length: _____ blocks

$$\begin{array}{r} 7 \\ + 4 \\ \hline 11 \end{array}$$

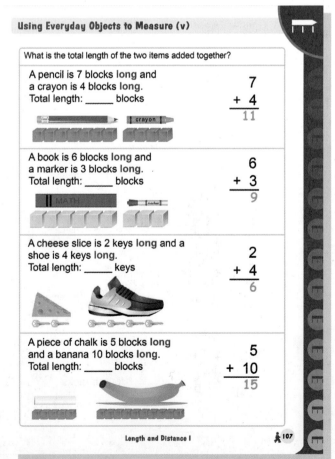

A book is 6 blocks **long** and a marker is 3 blocks **long**.
Total length: _____ blocks

$$\begin{array}{r} 6 \\ + 3 \\ \hline 9 \end{array}$$

A cheese slice is 2 keys **long** and a shoe is 4 keys **long**.
Total length: _____ keys

$$\begin{array}{r} 2 \\ + 4 \\ \hline 6 \end{array}$$

A piece of chalk is 5 blocks **long** and a banana 10 blocks **long**.
Total length: _____ blocks

$$\begin{array}{r} 5 \\ + 10 \\ \hline 15 \end{array}$$

Fill in the blank with the correct letter.

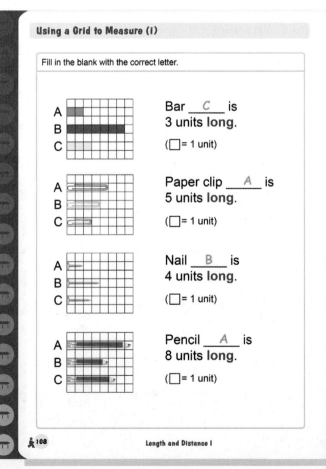

Bar _____C_____ is 3 units **long**.
(☐ = 1 unit)

Paper clip _____A_____ is 5 units **long**.
(☐ = 1 unit)

Nail _____B_____ is 4 units **long**.
(☐ = 1 unit)

Pencil _____A_____ is 8 units **long**.
(☐ = 1 unit)

Answer Key

Fill in the blank with the correct name.

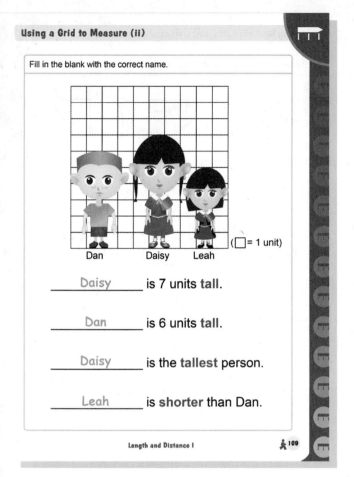

(☐ = 1 unit)

Dan   Daisy   Leah

_____Daisy_____ is 7 units **tall**.

_____Dan_____ is 6 units **tall**.

_____Daisy_____ is the **tallest** person.

_____Leah_____ is **shorter** than Dan.

Length and Distance I   109

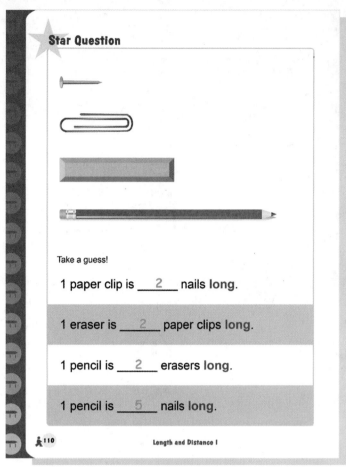

Take a guess!

1 paper clip is ___2___ nails **long**.

1 eraser is ___2___ paper clips **long**.

1 pencil is ___2___ erasers **long**.

1 pencil is ___5___ nails **long**.

110   *Length and Distance I*

Practice drawing curved lines and straight lines.

120   Straight Lines and Curved Lines

Draw a line around the object to complete each picture. Next to it, circle the word straight or curved to show what kind of line you drew.

straight
(curved)

(straight)
curved

straight
(curved)

straight
(curved)

Straight Lines and Curved Lines   121

Answer Key   157

Drawing Straight and Curved Lines (iii)

Draw a line around the object to complete each picture. Next to it, circle the word straight or curved to show what kind of line you drew.

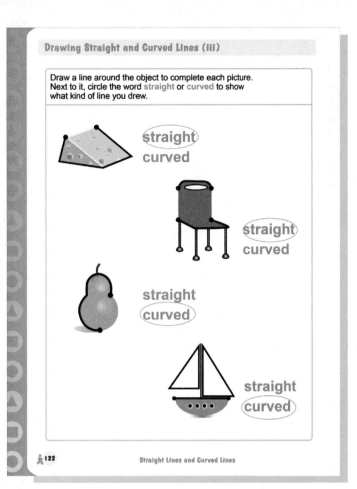

Finding Straight Lines and Curved Lines in Shapes (i)

Circle all the figures with at least one curved line.

Circle all the figures with at least one straight line.

Circle the figure with exactly 2 curved lines.

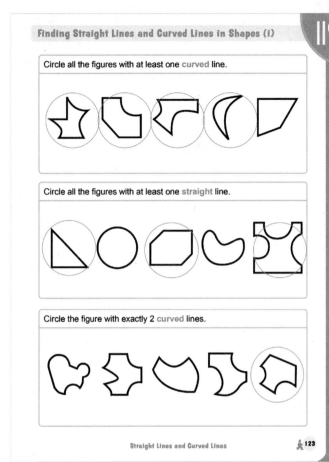

Finding Straight Lines and Curved Lines in Shapes (ii)

Draw a ○ under the figure(s) with only curved lines.

Draw a □ under the figure(s) with only straight lines.

Draw a ⌓ under the figure(s) with both curved lines and straight lines.

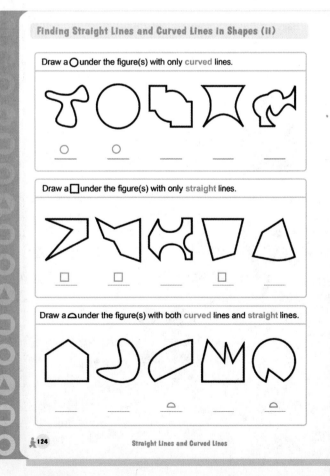

Finding Straight Lines and Curved Lines in Shapes (iii)

Color the figures with curved lines red.
Color the figures with straight lines blue.

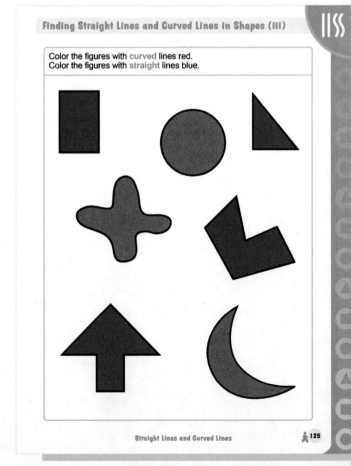

Answer Key

How many straight lines are there on each shape?

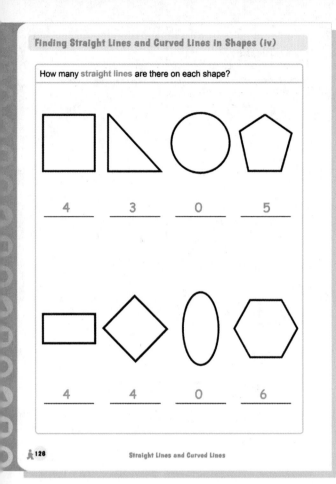

4   3   0   5

4   4   0   6

Trace to complete each shape. Did you draw curved lines or straight lines? Write your answers.

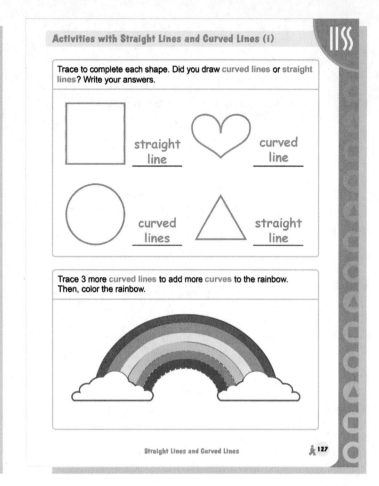

straight line

curved line

curved lines

straight line

Trace 3 more curved lines to add more curves to the rainbow. Then, color the rainbow.

Draw the following objects in the box. On the line, write whether the object has straight lines or curved lines or both.

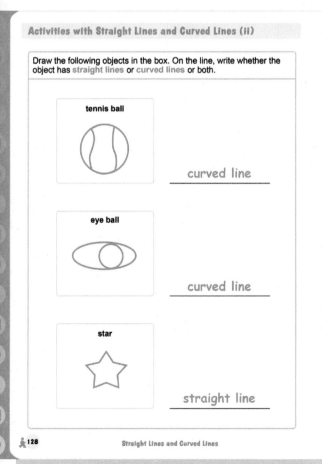

tennis ball

curved line

eye ball

curved line

star

straight line

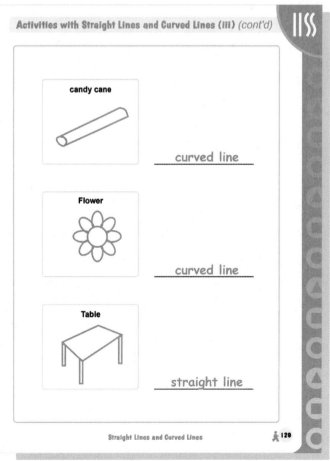

candy cane

curved line

Flower

curved line

Table

straight line

Answer Key   159

Draw your own closed shapes using:

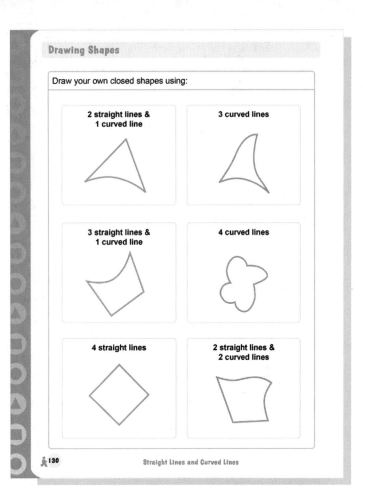

2 straight lines & 1 curved line	3 curved lines
3 straight lines & 1 curved line	4 curved lines
4 straight lines	2 straight lines & 2 curved lines

Star Question

Draw a straight line, a curved line, or a shape to complete each pattern.

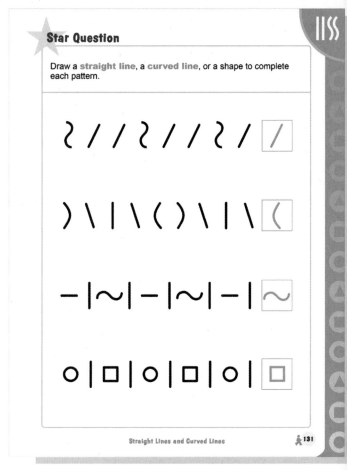

Answer Key

You did it!

Looking GOOD!

You ROCK!

You are # 1

AWESOME!

Fabulous!

You are building some super math skills!

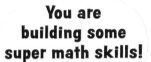

SUPER!

Way to stick with it!

WOO HOO!

Woof-tastic!

Awesome! What more can I say?

You are a math champ!

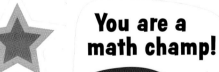